Better Homes and Gardens®

COOKING
for
TWO

Better Homes and Gardens®

COOKING
for
TWO

©1968 by Meredith Corporation, Des Moines, Iowa.
All Rights Reserved. Printed in the United States of America.
First Edition. Eighteenth Printing, 1980.
Library of Congress Catalog Card Number: 73-185
ISBN: 0-696-00450-X

CONTENTS

On our cover: Hearty Ham-broccoli Rolls have vegetable and meat all wrapped up in individual bundles. Top off the meal with Oranges Piquant—a petite dessert made just for two.

Better Homes and Gardens TEST KITCHEN ®

Our checked seal assures you that every recipe in *Cooking for Two* is tested and endorsed by the Better Homes and Gardens Test Kitchen.

FRANKLY FANCY— JUST FOR TWO

Cooking for two can be creative, as this chapter will illustrate. Whether you're celebrating your husband's promotion, planning a birthday dinner for your roommate, or entertaining a special friend for brunch, you'll find the perfect meal for the occasion.

We've included detailed directions for Beef Fondue—a delightfully easy way to serve an elegant, intimate dinner for two. There's also a low-calorie dinner with foods so luscious no one will know you're weight watching.

If you're a novice cook or your family has grown and you're once again a twosome, these recipes will make cooking for two rewarding. When you want to make that just-right impression or have reason to celebrate, turn here for foods with emphasis on the extra-special. It's those extra touches—special sauces, savory stuffings, inviting appetizers, pretty garnishes—that make a meal an occasion.

Feature Cornish Game Hens with Rice Stuffing at your next dinner for two. Serve with Spicy Cranberries in lemon cups and Raspberry-melon Boats.

⋞ MENU ⋟

Candlelight Dinner

Savory Tomato Soup
Cornish Game Hens with Rice Stuffing
Buttered Brussels Sprouts
Spicy Cranberries   Hard Rolls
Raspberry-melon Boats
White Wine
Coffee

CORNISH GAME HENS WITH RICE STUFFING

    2 1-pound Cornish game hens
      Salt
      Pepper
      • • •
    2 tablespoons slivered almonds
    2 tablespoons finely chopped onion
    ⅓ cup uncooked long-grain rice
    3 tablespoons butter or margarine
      • • •
    1 cup water
    1 chicken bouillon cube
    1 teaspoon lemon juice
    ½ teaspoon salt
    1 3-ounce can chopped mushrooms,
      drained (½ cup)

Season game hens inside and out with salt and pepper. In small saucepan, cook almonds, onion, and rice in butter for 5 to 10 minutes, stirring frequently.

Add water, bouillon cube, lemon juice, and salt. Bring mixture to boiling, stirring to dissolve bouillon cube. Reduce heat; cover and cook slowly about 20 to 25 minutes or till liquid is absorbed and rice is fluffy. Stir in the drained mushrooms.

Lightly stuff birds with rice mixture. Place breast up on rack in shallow baking pan. Brush with melted butter or margarine. Roast covered in hot oven (400°) for 30 minutes. Uncover and roast 1 hour longer or till drumstick can be twisted easily in socket. Brush birds with melted butter during last 15 minutes of roasting time. Makes 2 servings.

SAVORY TOMATO SOUP

    ¼ cup chopped celery
    2 tablespoons chopped green onion
    1 tablespoon butter or margarine
    2 teaspoons all-purpose flour
      • • •
    1 8-ounce can stewed tomatoes
    1 cup water
    ¼ cup dry white wine *or* water
    1 chicken bouillon cube
    2 slices crisp-cooked bacon, crumbled

Cook celery and onion in butter till tender but not brown. Blend in flour. Add remaining ingredients, except bacon; cook and stir till slightly thick. Reduce heat; cook slowly 15 minutes, stirring occasionally. Garnish with bacon. Makes 2 servings.

SPICY CRANBERRIES

    ½ cup sugar
    2 inches stick cinnamon
    1 cup fresh cranberries

Combine ¼ cup water and sugar in small saucepan. Add cinnamon. Bring to boil, stirring till sugar dissolves. Add cranberries and boil rapidly till berries just pop, about 2 minutes. Chill. Remove cinnamon. Serve in hollowed out lemon cups. Makes ¾ cup.

RASPBERRY-MELON BOATS

    1 10-ounce package frozen red
      raspberries, thawed
    ½ cup orange juice
    1 tablespoon cornstarch
    1 tablespoon sugar
    1 small cantaloupe, chilled
      Vanilla ice cream

Drain raspberries, reserving ½ cup syrup. To syrup, add orange juice. In small saucepan, mix cornstarch and sugar; gradually stir in raspberry-orange syrup. Bring to boiling, stirring constantly; cook till thick and bubbly. Cool sauce; add drained raspberries.

Halve melon; remove seeds and rind. Fill centers with scoops of vanilla ice cream. Drizzle with raspberry sauce. Makes 2 servings.

To broil lobster, "butterfly" tails with a French knife. Broil with meat side up.

To serve lobster tails, loosen meat by inserting fork between the shell and meat.

EASY GRASSHOPPER PIE

½ cup chocolate-wafer crumbs
1 tablespoon butter or margarine, melted

• • •

½ 1-pint jar marshmallow creme
1 tablespoon green creme de menthe
1 tablespoon white creme de cacao
½ cup whipping cream, whipped

Combine wafer crumbs and butter or margarine; press into two 4¼-inch tart pans.

In small mixer bowl, combine marshmallow creme and liqueurs. Beat about 1 minute at high speed. Fold in whipped cream. Pile into crumb crust. Freeze about 5 hours or overnight. If desired, garnish with additional whipped cream. Makes 2 servings.

Celebration Night

Chilled Fruit Cup
Broiled Lobster Tails
Drawn Butter   Lemon Butter
Parslied New Potatoes
Mixed Greens   Blue Cheese Dressing
Easy Grasshopper Pie
Coffee

BROILED LOBSTER TAILS

Place 4 frozen 6- or 8-ounce rock lobster tails on cutting board. With large sharp knife, cut down through center of hard top shell, cutting through meat but not through under membrane. Spread open, butterfly-style, so meat is on top. Cover tail fans with foil. Brush meat with melted butter. Broil 4 inches from heat about 17 minutes. Brush often with butter. Meat is done when it loses its translucency and can be flaked with a fork. Serves 2.

PARSLIED NEW POTATOES

¾ pound tiny new potatoes
2 tablespoons butter or margarine
2 tablespoons snipped parsley
1½ teaspoons lemon juice

Scrub or scrape potatoes. Cook in boiling salted water till tender, 15 to 20 minutes. Drain. Peel if desired. Meanwhile, melt butter in saucepan; stir in parsley and lemon juice. Pour over hot potatoes. Serves 2 or 3.

BLUE CHEESE DRESSING

Have 2 ounces blue cheese, crumbled (½ cup) at room temperature. Blend in ¼ cup mayonnaise or salad dressing. Gradually stir in ½ cup buttermilk, mixing thoroughly. Cover; chill. Makes 1 cup dressing.

TOASTY FRENCH SLICES

Bread toasts in oven while chicken bakes—

    4 1-inch slices French bread
    3 tablespoons butter, softened
    1 tablespoon grated Parmesan
       cheese

Spread French bread with softened butter on both sides. Arrange in a 12x8x2-inch baking dish. Sprinkle slices with Parmesan cheese. Bake at 375° about 15 minutes or till toasty and golden brown. Makes 2 servings.

❧ MENU ❧

Chicken Dinner for Two

Cream of Celery Soup
Curried Orange Chicken
Buttered Asparagus
Fresh Fruit Salad   Mayonnaise
Toasty French Slices
Chocolate Sponge Cake   Ice Cream
Coffee

CURRIED ORANGE CHICKEN

Curry fans might like 1 teaspoon curry—

    1 2-pound ready-to-cook broiler-fryer
      chicken, cut up
  ½ teaspoon curry powder
  ¼ cup orange juice
    2 tablespoons honey
    1 tablespoon prepared mustard
    2 teaspoons cornstarch
    1 tablespoon cold water
  ½ orange, peeled, sliced, and
      quartered

Sprinkle chicken pieces with curry powder; rub curry into meat. Arrange chicken in small baking dish, skin side down. Combine orange juice, honey, and mustard in small saucepan; simmer till blended. Pour over chicken; bake in moderate oven (375°) for 30 minutes. Turn chicken and continue baking 20 minutes longer or till tender.

Remove chicken to serving platter; keep warm. In small saucepan, combine cornstarch and water; stir in pan juices from chicken. Cook and stir till thick and bubbly. Add orange pieces; heat 1 minute. Pour sauce over chicken on platter or serve separately to be spooned over hot cooked rice. Makes 2 servings.

POT ROAST DINNER

Weight-watchers: a dinner just for you—

  ¾ pound boneless beef chuck roast
    1 teaspoon salad oil
  ½ teaspoon salt
      Dash pepper
  ¾ cup water
    2 carrots, pared and halved
    1 small onion, peeled, quartered
    2 medium potatoes, pared and
      quartered

In heavy skillet, brown meat slowly on all sides in hot oil. Season with salt and pepper. Add water; cover and simmer for 1 hour, adding water if necessary. Add carrots, onion, and potatoes. Continue to simmer 45 to 60 minutes longer or till vegetables and meat are tender. Serve with skimmed pan juices (do not thicken). Trim with parsley. Serves 2.

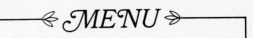

MENU

Low-cal and Luscious

Saucy Chicken Breasts
Italian Green Beans
Slim-jim Salad Molds
Bread Sticks
Fresh Fruit
Coffee

SAUCY CHICKEN BREASTS

    2 small whole chicken breasts, split
      in halves
  ¼ teaspoon seasoned salt
      Paprika
    1 chicken bouillon cube
    2 tablespoons sauterne *or* water
  ¼ teaspoon instant minced onion
  ¼ teaspoon curry powder
    1 2-ounce can sliced mushrooms

Sprinkle chicken with seasoned salt and paprika; place in small baking dish. Dissolve bouillon cube in ⅔ cup boiling water. Add wine, onion, curry, and dash pepper; pour over chicken. Cover; bake at 350° for 30 minutes. Uncover; bake 45 minutes or till tender.

Remove chicken to platter. Blend 1 tablespoon flour and 2 tablespoons cold water in saucepan; stir in pan juices. Cook and stir till bubbly. Drain mushrooms; add to gravy; heat through. Spoon over chicken. Serves 2.

SLIM-JIM SALAD MOLDS

    1 4-serving envelope lemon-flavored
      low-calorie gelatin
    1 tablespoon vinegar
  ½ cup shredded carrot
    1 tablespoon chopped green onion

Combine gelatin and dash salt; add 2 cups boiling water and vinegar; stir till gelatin dissolves. Chill till partially set; fold in carrot and onion. Pour into 4 individual molds. Chill firm. Unmold on greens. Serves 4.

PEPPY POTATO SALAD

¼ teaspoon mustard seed
¼ teaspoon dillseed
1 tablespoon water
1½ cups diced cooked potatoes
1 tablespoon sliced green onion
2 tablespoons thinly sliced celery
1 hard-cooked egg, chopped
¼ cup Zippy Cooked Dressing

Soak mustard seed and dillseed in water several hours or overnight. Combine seed-water mixture and ½ teaspoon salt. Add potatoes, onion, and celery; mix lightly. Add egg and ¼ cup Dressing; toss to coat. Chill thoroughly. Garnish with radish roses. Makes 2 servings.

Zippy Cooked Dressing: In small saucepan, mix 1 tablespoon all-purpose flour, 1 tablespoon sugar, ½ teaspoon salt, ½ teaspoon dry mustard, and dash cayenne.

Gradually stir in 1 slightly beaten egg yolk and ⅓ cup milk. Cook and stir over medium heat till mixture thickens and boils. Remove from heat; stir in 2 tablespoons vinegar and 1 teaspoon butter. Cover; cool. Makes ½ cup.

Note: Make Thousand Island Dressing from remaining cooked dressing stirring in 1 tablespoon chili sauce and 1 teaspoon pickle relish; serve over lettuce another time.

Peppy Potato Salad—extraordinary

Here's potato salad to make you sit up and take notice! You perk up that old-time flavor with mustard seed and dillseed.

CHARCOAL-BROILED STEAK

Select Porterhouse, T-bone, Club, Sirloin, or Tenderloin (filet mignon) steak cut about 1 inch thick. (Allow about 2 servings per pound.) Slash fat edge at 1-inch intervals. Put steaks on hot, greased grill. Broil 1-inch-thick steaks over hot coals allowing 4 to 5 minutes per side for rare, 7 to 8 minutes per side for medium, and 10 to 11 minutes per side for well done. Flip steaks with tongs. Season with salt and pepper. Test doneness by cutting next to bone. Pass Sauce Provencale.

SAUCE PROVENCALE

   1 medium tomato, peeled, cut in
      6 to 8 wedges, and seeded
   ¼ teaspoon sugar
            • • •
   2 teaspoons butter or margarine
   1 tablespoon chopped green onion
   2 tablespoons dry sherry
   2 tablespoons butter or margarine
   1 small clove garlic, minced
   2 teaspoons snipped parsley

Sprinkle tomato wedges with sugar; set aside. Melt the 2 teaspoons butter in skillet. Add green onion; heat through. Add wine; cook and stir till liquid is slightly reduced. Add tomato; heat through. (Do not allow wedges to lose shape.) Add remaining ingredients. Heat, stirring gently, till butter melts. Season to taste with salt and pepper. Serve over Charcoal-broiled Steak. Makes 1 cup.

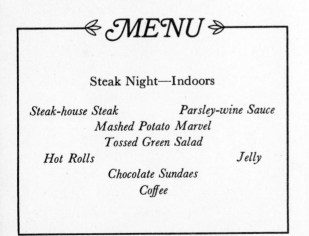

❧ MENU ❧

Steak Night—Indoors

Steak-house Steak   Parsley-wine Sauce
      Mashed Potato Marvel
          Tossed Green Salad
Hot Rolls   Jelly
          Chocolate Sundaes
               Coffee

STEAK-HOUSE STEAK

Choose tender steaks such as Sirloin, T-bone, Rib, Tenderloin, or Porterhouse. Steaks should be at least 1 inch thick for best flavor. Slash fat edge of steak at 1-inch intervals to prevent meat from curling as it broils. Place on cold rack in broiler pan. Broil 1- to 1½-inch steaks so surface of meat is 3 inches from source of heat, thicker cuts 4 to 5 inches from heat. Broil to desired doneness, turning steak only once. Use tongs to turn meat so juices don't escape. Pass Parsley-wine Sauce.

Thickness of steak	Rare	Medium (total time in minutes)	Well-done
1-inch	8 to 10	12 to 14	18 to 20
1½-inch	14 to 16	18 to 20	25 to 30
2-inch	20 to 25	30 to 35	40 to 45

PARSLEY-WINE SAUCE

In small saucepan, combine 1 tablespoon finely chopped onion and ⅓ cup dry white wine. Cook till wine is reduced by half. Remove from heat and stir in 3 tablespoons butter, 1 tablespoon snipped parsley, and dash *each* salt and pepper. Serve with steak.

MASHED POTATO MARVEL

   2 medium potatoes, pared and
      cut in pieces
   1 3-ounce package cream cheese,
      softened
   3 tablespoons light cream
   ½ teaspoon salt
      Dash pepper
      Dash fines herbes
   1 tablespoon butter or margarine

Cook potatoes in boiling salted water till tender; drain. Beat cream cheese till fluffy. Add hot potatoes gradually, beating constantly till light and fluffy. Beat in cream. Season with salt, pepper, and fines herbes. Pile in two mounds on greased heavy-duty aluminum foil. Dot with butter or margarine. Broil with steak last 5 minutes. Makes 2 servings.

MENU

Italian Night

Individual Antipasto Plates
Mixed Greens   Oil and Vinegar
Bread Sticks
Two-way Tortoni
Red Wine
Coffee

ANTIPASTO

Arrange some or all of following on plates: chilled tuna in lettuce cups, cheese wedges, pepperoni slices, olives, radish roses, pickled peppers, honeydew balls with prosciutto ham, cherry tomatoes, marinated artichoke hearts.

TWO-WAY TORTONI

- ½ cup whipping cream
- ¼ cup sugar
- ½ teaspoon vanilla
- 2 drops almond extract
- 1 egg white
- 2 tablespoons finely chopped almonds, toasted
- 2 tablespoons coconut, toasted
- ½ teaspoon instant coffee powder

Whip cream with 2 *tablespoons* sugar, vanilla, and extract. Beat white to soft peaks. Gradually add remaining sugar; beat to stiff peaks. Mix almonds and coconut. Fold white and *half* the nut mixture into cream; spoon half into 2 paper bake cups in muffin pan. Stir coffee powder into remaining whipped cream mixture. Spoon into 2 bake cups. Sprinkle remaining nut mixture over all. Freeze. Serves 4.

Make a meal of antipasto

Though antipasto means "before the pasta," this hearty array of food, meant to serve one, could easily be the main course.

The Meal on Our Cover

Ham-broccoli Rolls
Pineapple Rings   *Spiced Crab Apples*
Croissants   *Butter*
Oranges Piquant
Peanut Butter Puffs
Coffee

HAM-BROCCOLI ROLLS

2 rectangular slices boiled ham, cut ¼ inch thick
2 slices process Swiss cheese
1 10-ounce package frozen broccoli spears, cooked and drained

• • •

1½ teaspoons butter or margarine
1½ teaspoons all-purpose flour
⅛ teaspoon salt
1½ teaspoons prepared horseradish
1 teaspoon prepared mustard
¼ teaspoon Worcestershire sauce
¼ teaspoon grated onion

• • •

1 slightly beaten egg yolk
½ cup pineapple juice
¼ cup milk

Top each ham slice with slice of cheese. Place *half* the cooked broccoli on each. In heavy saucepan, melt butter. Blend in flour, salt, horseradish, mustard, Worcestershire sauce, and onion. Combine egg yolk and pineapple juice; blend into butter mixture. Stir in milk. Cook over low heat, stirring constantly, till thick and bubbling.

Spoon about 1 tablespoon sauce over broccoli. Roll ham and cheese around broccoli; secure with wooden picks. Place rolls in shallow baking dish. Cover; bake in moderate oven (350°) about 25 minutes.

Reheat remaining sauce, adding milk if necessary. Spoon hot mustard sauce over ham rolls. Garnish with pineapple slices and spiced crab apples. Makes 2 servings.

ORANGES PIQUANT

1 11-ounce can mandarin oranges, chilled
2 tablespoons orange marmalade
2 to 3 tablespoons dairy sour cream

Drain oranges, reserving 1 tablespoon syrup. Combine reserved syrup and marmalade; heat till marmalade melts. Place oranges in 2 dessert dishes; spoon marmalade over. Trim each with a dollop of sour cream. Serves 2.

PEANUT BUTTER PUFFS

1 egg white
Dash salt
6 tablespoons sugar
¼ cup peanut butter

In small mixer bowl, beat egg white with salt till soft peaks form. Gradually add sugar, beating till stiff peaks form. Stir in peanut butter. Drop from teaspoon 1 inch apart on greased cookie sheet. Bake in a slow oven (325°) for 18 minutes or till lightly browned. Cool slightly before removing from pan to cooling rack. Makes 1 dozen cookies.

LEMON SAUCE

¼ cup sugar
2 teaspoons cornstarch
Dash salt
Dash ground nutmeg
½ cup cold water

• • •

1 beaten egg yolk
1 tablespoon butter or margarine
¼ teaspoon grated lemon peel
1 tablespoon lemon juice

In small saucepan, combine sugar, cornstarch, salt, and nutmeg. Stir in water. Cook and stir over low heat till mixture thickens and bubbles. Stir small amount hot mixture into beaten egg yolk; return to hot mixture; cook and stir 1 minute longer.

Remove from heat. Add butter, lemon peel, and lemon juice; blend thoroughly. Serve over angel cake. Makes about ½ cup sauce.

APPLE-LIME COOLER

½ pint lime sherbet
¾ cup apple juice, chilled

Beat sherbet till softened and smooth. Gradually stir in apple juice till mixture is blended. Pour into 2 chilled glasses; serve at once.

LOBSTER EN CASSEROLE

2 tablespoons chopped onion
½ clove garlic, minced
1 tablespoon butter or margarine
½ 11-ounce can condensed Cheddar cheese soup (about ⅔ cup)
1 3-ounce can sliced mushrooms, drained
¼ cup milk
2 tablespoons dry sherry
1 tablespoon snipped parsley
1½ cups canned *or* fresh *or* frozen cooked lobster
½ cup frozen peas, cooked and drained
1 tablespoon buttered soft bread crumbs

Cook onion and garlic in butter till tender but not brown. Stir in soup and mushrooms. Gradually blend in milk, wine, and parsley. Add lobster and peas. Cook and stir till heated through. Spoon into two 1-cup casseroles; top each with a wreath of crumbs. Bake in a moderate oven (350°) for 25 to 30 minutes. Makes 2 servings.

⋠ *MENU* ⋗

Seafood Special

Apple-lime Cooler
Lobster en Casserole
or
Scallops Mornay
Green Beans   *Mixed Fruit Mold*
Hard Rolls   *Butter*
Angel Cake Slices   *Lemon Sauce*
Coffee

SCALLOPS MORNAY

½ cup sauterne
¾ cup water
¼ teaspoon salt
Dash pepper
¼ teaspoon instant minced onion
• • •
8 ounces frozen scallops (halve or quarter if large), about 1½ cups
½ cup sliced fresh mushrooms
• • •
1 tablespoon butter or margarine
1½ tablespoons all-purpose flour
½ cup milk
¼ cup grated process Swiss cheese
1 to 2 tablespoons snipped parsley

Combine wine, water, salt, pepper, and instant onion in saucepan; simmer 5 minutes. Add scallops and mushrooms; cover; simmer 5 minutes. Remove scallops and mushrooms; set aside while preparing sauce.

Cook stock in pan till reduced to ½ cup, about 15 minutes. Melt butter in another saucepan; stir in flour. Stir in fish stock and milk; cook and stir till mixture thickens and bubbles. Add cheese, stirring till melted. Season with salt and pepper, if needed.

Remove from heat; add scallops and mushrooms. Spoon into two individual baking dishes. Bake in moderate oven (375°) for 15 to 20 minutes. Trim with parsley. Serves 2.

MIXED FRUIT MOLD

1 12-ounce package frozen mixed fruit, thawed
1 3-ounce package raspberry-flavored gelatin
1 7-ounce bottle lemon-lime carbonated beverage (about 1 cup)

Drain mixed fruit, reserving syrup. Add enough water to syrup to make 1 cup. Heat to boiling; add gelatin; stir till dissolved. Cool to room temperature; gently stir in carbonated beverage. Chill till partially set. Fold in fruit. Pour into 9x5x3-inch loaf pan. Chill till firm.

Cut in squares; serve on salad greens. Top each serving with a dollop of mayonnaise or salad dressing. Makes 3 or 4 servings.

MENU

Anniversary Dinner

Beef Fondue

Blue Cheese Sauce   *Red Sauce*

Caper Butter   *Bordelaise Sauce*

Mixed Green Salad

Herb-buttered Rolls

Mocha-mallow Parfaits

Red Wine   *Coffee*

BEEF FONDUE

Salad oil
¾   pound trimmed beef tenderloin,
cut in ¾-inch cubes

Heat oil in saucepan to 425° on range (do not let oil smoke). Pour oil into fondue cooker to no more than ½ capacity or to depth of about 2 inches. Place over canned heat or alcohol burner. Have beef cubes at room temperature in serving bowl. Set out small bowls of several or all of the sauces in the menu.

Spear beef cube on fondue fork and hold in hot oil till cooked to desired doneness. Transfer cooked beef to dinner fork and dip in one of the sauces on plate. Makes 2 servings.

BLUE CHEESE SAUCE

½   cup dairy sour cream
2   tablespoons crumbled blue
cheese
Dash Worcestershire sauce

Combine all ingredients; chill well.

RED SAUCE

⅓   cup catsup
1   tablespoon vinegar
¼   teaspoon prepared horseradish

Combine catsup, vinegar, and horseradish till blended; chill. Makes about ⅓ cup.

CAPER BUTTER

¼   cup butter, softened
1½   tablespoons capers with liquid

In small mixer bowl, combine butter and capers with liquid; beat till light and fluffy.

BORDELAISE SAUCE

¼   cup chopped fresh mushrooms
2   teaspoons butter or margarine
1½   tablespoons cornstarch
1   cup cold beef broth
1½   tablespoons red wine
1   tablespoon lemon juice
1   teaspoon dried tarragon,
crushed

In small saucepan, cook mushrooms in butter till tender, about 4 minutes. Combine cornstarch and beef broth. Blend into mushrooms. Cook and stir till mixture boils. Add remaining ingredients and dash pepper. Simmer about 5 minutes. Makes about 1 cup.

HERB-BUTTERED ROLLS

Combine ¼ cup softened butter, 1½ teaspoons finely snipped green onion, 1½ teaspoons finely snipped parsley, and ⅛ to ¼ teaspoon dried rosemary, crushed. Spread on cut surfaces of 3 hard rolls, halved. Wrap in foil; heat at 350° for 10 minutes or till hot.

MOCHA-MALLOW PARFAITS

12   marshmallows (about 1½ cups)
1½   teaspoons instant coffee powder
½   cup whipping cream, whipped
¼   cup chocolate-wafer crumbs

In small saucepan, combine marshmallows, ½ cup water, and coffee powder. Cook and stir over medium heat till marshmallows are melted. Chill till partially set; fold in whipped cream. (If mixture thins, chill about 20 minutes or till partially set again.)

In parfait glasses, alternate layers of coffee mixture and wafer crumbs, beginning and ending with coffee mixture. Serves 2.

⟨ MENU ⟩

Birthday Party for Two

One-rib Broil
Fresh Mushroom Saute
Lettuce Wedge   *French Dressing*
Spicy Crunch Muffins   *Butter*
Mint Patty Alaskas
Red Wine   *Coffee*

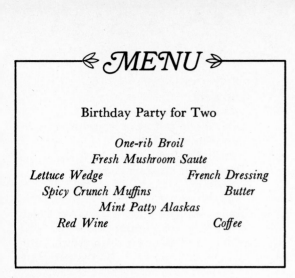

ONE-RIB BROIL

Slash fat edge at 1-inch intervals of a 1-rib beef rib roast, 2 inches thick. Broil 5 inches from heat for 35 to 40 minutes for medium to medium-well done meat. Turn once during broiling. Cut into 2 servings.

FRESH MUSHROOM SAUTE

  1 pint mushrooms (about ½ pound)
  3 tablespoons butter or margarine
  2 teaspoons all-purpose flour

Wash mushrooms. Slice lengthwise through cap and stem. Melt butter in skillet. Add mushrooms. Sprinkle with flour; toss to coat. Cover and cook over low heat till tender, 8 to 10 minutes, turning occasionally. Season with salt and pepper. Makes 2 servings.

SPICY CRUNCH MUFFINS

Sift together into a bowl, 1 cup sifted all-purpose flour, 2 teaspoons baking powder, ½ teaspoon salt, ¼ teaspoon ground cinnamon, and ¼ teaspoon ground nutmeg. Stir ⅓ cup brown sugar and 2 tablespoons *finely* chopped walnuts into flour mixture.

Combine 1 beaten egg, ⅓ cup milk, and 2 tablespoons salad oil. Add all at once to dry ingredients, stirring just to blend. Fold in ⅓ cup whole wheat flakes. Fill 6 greased muffin pans ⅔ full. Bake in hot oven (400°) for 15 to 20 minutes. Makes 6 muffins.

Pretty Mint Patty Alaskas are quick to fix with little fuss. Peppermint ice cream patties stay cool under a fluffy meringue.

MINT PATTY ALASKAS

  2 egg whites
 ¼ teaspoon cream of tartar
 ¼ teaspoon vanilla
    Dash salt
 ¼ cup sugar
  2 sponge cake dessert cups
  2 chocolate-coated peppermint
    ice cream patties
  1 tablespoon crushed peppermint-stick
    candy

Beat egg whites with cream of tartar, vanilla, and salt to soft peaks. Gradually add sugar, beating to stiff peaks. Place cake cups on cutting board; top each with ice cream patty. Cover with meringue, spreading thicker over ice cream and thinner around cake; seal edges at bottom. Sprinkle meringue with candy. Bake at 500° for 2 to 3 minutes or till browned. Serve at once. Serves 2.

≪ *MENU* ≫

Sunday-best Dinner

Saucy Onion Chicken
Parslied Carrots
Lime-apple Squares
Crescent Rolls   *Butter*
Crumb-top Apple Pie (page 46)
Coffee

SAUCY ONION CHICKEN

2 small whole chicken breasts or
   1 large chicken breast, split
1 tablespoon butter or margarine
½ cup sauterne
   • • •
2 tablespoons water
¼ cup dairy sour cream French
   onion dip
   Hot cooked rice

Remove skin from chicken breasts. In small skillet, brown chicken in butter. Season with salt and pepper. Add sauterne. Cover and simmer for 20 to 25 minutes or till tender. Remove chicken; keep warm. Add water to skillet, scraping browned bits from bottom of pan. Stir in onion dip till well blended. To serve, arrange chicken on hot cooked rice and pour the sauce over all. Serves 2.

LIME-APPLE SQUARES

1 1-pound can (2 cups) applesauce
1 3-ounce package lime-flavored
   gelatin
1 7-ounce bottle lemon-
   lime carbonated beverage
   (about 1 cup)

In small saucepan, combine applesauce and gelatin; cook and stir till gelatin dissolves. Gently stir in lemon-lime beverage. Pour into 9x5x3-inch pan. Chill till firm. Cut in squares; serve on greens. Makes 4 to 6 servings.

PEANUT BUTTER PARFAITS

1 cup brown sugar
⅓ cup milk
¼ cup light corn syrup
1 tablespoon butter or margarine
¼ cup peanut butter
   Vanilla ice cream
   Peanuts *or* crushed peanut
   brittle

In medium saucepan, combine brown sugar, milk, corn syrup, and butter. Cook and stir over medium heat till sugar dissolves and butter melts; remove from heat. Add peanut butter; beat smooth with rotary beater; cool.

In parfait glasses, alternate layers of vanilla ice cream and peanut butter sauce, beginning and ending with ice cream. Garnish parfaits with peanuts or crushed peanut brittle, if desired. Makes 4 servings.

Hot Sherried Consomme is an easy but elegant appetizer. Pour consomme over silver spoon to prevent cracking of crystal glass.

MENU

Winter Night Special

Hot Sherried Consomme
Pork Loin Roast
Applesauce
Buttered Italian Green Beans
Blue Cheese Toss
Hard Rolls   *Butter*
Peanut Butter Parfaits
Coffee

HOT SHERRIED CONSOMME

In saucepan, combine one 10½-ounce can condensed consomme, ⅔ cup water, and 3 tablespoons dry sherry; heat. Serves 2.

PORK LOIN ROAST

Rub fat side of 3- to 5-pound pork loin roast with salt, pepper, and ground sage. Place fat side up on rack in open roasting pan. Insert meat thermometer in center of roast. Roast uncovered in slow oven (325°) for 2½ to 3 hours or till thermometer registers 170°.

BLUE CHEESE TOSS

¼ cup salad oil
2 tablespoons tarragon vinegar
½ teaspoon sugar
¼ teaspoon salt
⅛ teaspoon paprika
• • •
1 cup sliced raw cauliflowerets
½ cup thinly sliced Bermuda onion
2 tablespoons sliced pimiento-stuffed green olives
2 cups torn lettuce
1 ounce blue cheese, crumbled (¼ cup)

Mix first 5 ingredients. Combine cauliflower, onion rings, and olives; toss lightly with dressing. Cover; refrigerate 1 hour. Add lettuce and blue cheese; toss and serve. Serves 2 or 3.

Uses for leftover pork:

PORK CHOP SUEY

1 cup thin bias-cut celery slices
½ cup sliced onion
2 tablespoons butter or margarine
4 teaspoons cornstarch
2 tablespoons soy sauce
1 chicken bouillon cube
½ 5-ounce can water chestnuts, drained and sliced
1 cup cubed cooked pork
Hot cooked rice

In skillet, cook celery and onion in butter till tender-crisp, 2 to 3 minutes. Blend cornstarch into soy sauce. Dissolve bouillon cube in 1¼ cups boiling water. To skillet, add soy-cornstarch mixture, bouillon, water chestnuts, and pork. Cook and stir till thickened and bubbly. Serve over hot cooked rice. Serves 2.

BARBECUED PORK

3 tablespoons chopped onion
1 tablespoon butter or margarine
1 8-ounce can tomato sauce
2 tablespoons brown sugar
1 to 2 teaspoons Worcestershire sauce
1 teaspoon lemon juice
1 teaspoon prepared mustard
1 cup cubed cooked pork
2 hamburger buns, toasted

Cook onion in butter till tender. Add next 5 ingredients. Simmer about 20 minutes. Add cooked pork. Heat 10 minutes. Spoon sauce over bun halves. Serves 2.

CHOP CHOP SALAD

Toss together 3 cups thinly sliced Chinese cabbage, ¾ cup cold cooked rice, ⅔ cup cooked peas, 1 cup diced cooked pork, and ½ 5-ounce can water chestnuts, drained and sliced. Combine ¼ cup mayonnaise, ¼ cup dairy sour cream, ½ teaspoon celery seed, ½ teaspoon monosodium glutamate, and ¼ teaspoon salt; toss with salad. Chill. Makes 2 or 3 main-dish salad servings.

❦ MENU ❧

Chilly Morning Breakfast

Sliced Oranges
Spicy Raisin Oatmeal
or
Hot Whole Wheat Cereal   *Honey Butter*
Crisp Bacon   *Toast*
Coffee

SPICY RAISIN OATMEAL

1½ cups cold water
¼ cup raisins
½ teaspoon salt
¼ teaspoon ground cinnamon
⅛ teaspoon ground nutmeg
⅔ cup quick-cooking rolled oats

Combine water, raisins, salt, ground cinnamon and nutmeg in saucepan; bring to boiling. Slowly stir in rolled oats, making sure water continues to boil. Reduce heat and cook 1 minute, stirring occasionally.

Turn off heat; cover oatmeal and let stand 5 minutes. Serve hot with sugar and light cream or milk. Makes 2 servings.

HOT WHOLE WHEAT CEREAL

2¼ cups cold water
½ teaspoon salt
½ cup quick-cooking whole wheat
     cereal
· · ·
¼ cup butter, softened
¼ cup honey

Bring water to rapid boil; add salt. Gradually sprinkle in whole wheat cereal, making sure water continues to boil, stirring all the time. Reduce heat and boil gently 5 to 6 minutes, stirring occasionally. Serve with Honey Butter. Makes 2 servings.

Honey Butter: Whip butter till fluffy. Slowly add honey, beating till smooth.

BRUNCH FLOATS

For each serving, put a small scoop of lemon sherbet into bottom of 6-ounce juice glass. To each add about ⅓ cup orange juice and then 2 tablespoons lemon-lime carbonated beverage. Trim with orange slices. Serve at once.

NO-FLIP OVEN PANCAKE

Not really like the familiar flapjack but more of a puffy egg dish—

3 eggs
½ cup sifted all-purpose flour
¼ teaspoon salt
½ cup milk
2 tablespoons butter or margarine,
    melted
· · ·
2 tablespoons sugar
2 tablespoons sliced almonds,
    toasted
· · ·
1 tablespoon butter or margarine,
    melted
1 tablespoon lemon juice

Beat eggs till well blended. Slowly add flour, beating constantly. Stir in salt, milk, and the 2 tablespoons melted butter. Grease 10-inch skillet (handle must be removable or oven-proof). Pour batter into cool skillet.

Bake in a hot oven (400°) for 15 minutes or till pancake is browned and puffy. Remove from oven; quickly sprinkle with the sugar and toasted almonds. Combine the remaining tablespoon melted butter and the lemon juice; quickly drizzle over all. Serve pancake immediately. Makes 2 servings.

❦ MENU ❧

Pancake Brunch

Brunch Floats   or   Strawberry Starter
No-flip Oven Pancake
Sausage Links
Toasted English Muffins
Coffee

Leisurely Sunday Brunch

Orange-apricot Wake-up
Poached Eggs
Canadian-style Bacon
Miniature Brunch Loaf
Mexican Chocolate

STRAWBERRY STARTER

Rinse, hull, and halve fresh strawberries. Spoon into sherbet dishes. Combine ½ cup strawberry-flavored yogurt, 2 tablespoons sugar, and few drops red food coloring. Drizzle over berries. Garnish with mint sprigs.

ORANGE-APRICOT WAKE-UP

Combine equal parts chilled apricot nectar and orange juice in 6-ounce juice glasses. Add maraschino cherry to each.

MINIATURE BRUNCH LOAF

  2 tablespoons chopped pecans
  3 tablespoons brown sugar
  1 cup packaged biscuit mix
  ¼ teaspoon ground cinnamon
  ⅛ teaspoon ground mace
  3 tablespoons milk
  1 egg
  2 tablespoons butter, melted
  ¼ teaspoon vanilla

Mix pecans with 2 *tablespoons* brown sugar; set aside. Combine the biscuit mix, remaining 1 *tablespoon* brown sugar, and spices. Combine milk, egg, 1 *tablespoon* of the melted butter, and vanilla. Make a well in the center of dry ingredients; add liquid all at once.

Stir with fork till blended. Spoon *half* of the biscuit mixture into greased 5½x3x2¼-inch loaf pan; brush with *some* of the remaining butter and sprinkle with *half* of the pecan mixture. Repeat with remainder of the biscuit mixture, butter, and pecans. Bake at (350°) for 25 to 30 minutes. Serve warm.

MEXICAN CHOCOLATE

  2 cups milk
  2½ squares (2½ ounces) semisweet chocolate, broken up
  3 inches stick cinnamon
  ½ teaspoon vanilla

In small saucepan, combine the milk, semi-sweet chocolate, and stick cinnamon. Cook over medium heat, stirring constantly, till chocolate melts and mixture is heated through. Remove from heat and add the vanilla.

Remove cinnamon stick. Beat mixture vigorously with "molinillo" or rotary beater. Serve in warmed mugs. Makes 2 servings.

Mexican Chocolate gets a foamy crown when you beat it with an authentic "molinillo" (Mexican handmill) or rotary beater.

PECAN CHICKEN A LA KING

2 tablespoons butter or margarine
¼ cup chopped celery
1 chicken bouillon cube
2 tablespoons all-purpose flour
¼ teaspoon salt
⅛ teaspoon poultry seasoning
1¼ cups milk
1 teaspoon lemon juice
1 cup cubed cooked chicken
1 tablespoon chopped canned pimiento
¼ cup coarsely chopped pecans

In medium saucepan, melt butter; cook celery in butter till tender. Add bouillon cube; crush with back of spoon. Stir in flour, salt, and poultry seasoning. Add milk all at once. Cook, stirring constantly, till mixture thickens and bubbles.

Stir in lemon juice, chicken, pimiento, and all but a few of the pecans. Cook and stir till mixture is heated through. Spoon creamed chicken over warm waffles. Garnish with remaining pecans. Makes 2 servings.

HOT BUTTERED APRICOTS

1 tablespoon butter or margarine
1 8-ounce can apricots, drained
  Ground nutmeg

Melt butter in small skillet. Add apricots. Heat 3 to 4 minutes. Sprinkle lightly with ground nutmeg. Serve warm with waffles.

PERFECT WAFFLES

½ cup sifted all-purpose flour
½ teaspoon baking powder
  Dash salt
• • •
1 beaten egg yolk
½ cup milk
1 tablespoon salad oil
1 stiffly beaten egg white

Sift together flour, baking powder, and salt. Combine egg yolk and milk; stir into dry ingredients. Blend in salad oil. Fold in egg white, leaving a few fluffs—don't overmix. Bake in a preheated waffle baker according to manufacturer's directions. Makes 1 large waffle (4 individual squares).

Note: For a hurry-up waffle breakfast another time, bake extra waffles and freeze in packages. To thaw and heat, place in toaster.

DELUXE CREAMED EGGS

Deviled ham gives creamed eggs real zip—

4 crisp rusks
1 2¼-ounce can deviled ham
2 hard-cooked eggs
• • •
2 tablespoons butter or margarine
1 tablespoon finely chopped onion
2 tablespoons all-purpose flour
¼ teaspoon salt
1 cup milk
  Dash Worcestershire sauce
1 2-ounce can sliced mushrooms, drained

Spread tops of rusks with deviled ham. Heat rusks in slow oven (325°) for about 10 minutes. Slice one of the hard-cooked eggs, reserving 4 slices for garnish. Chop remaining egg slices and second whole egg.

Melt butter in saucepan. Add onion; cook till onion is tender but not brown. Blend in flour and salt. Add milk all at once along with the Worcestershire sauce. Cook, stirring constantly, till mixture thickens and bubbles.

Stir in chopped eggs and mushrooms. Cook and stir till mixture is heated through. Spoon over rusks. Trim with reserved egg slices; sprinkle with paprika. Makes 2 servings.

Pecan Chicken a la King is marvelous for brunch or as a supper entree. It's an elegant creamed mixture ladled over crisp waffles.

For an attractive plate mate, sweet apricot halves are heated in butter, then lightly dusted with nutmeg. Trim with parsley.

SPICY ORANGE TEA

        5 whole cloves
        1 inch stick cinnamon
        3 tablespoons honey
        ½ cup orange juice
        2 tea bags
           Bitters

Combine ½ cup water with cloves and cinnamon; simmer, covered, 10 minutes. Add honey, ½ cup water, and the orange juice; bring to boiling. Remove from heat; add tea bags. Cover and let stand 5 minutes; remove tea bags and spices. Dash in bitters. Serves 2.

Start breakfast with one of these:

• A compote of prunes and dried apricots cooked together with *thin* slices of lemon.
• Chilled orange slices capped with a generous fluff of shredded coconut.
• Fresh or frozen blueberries sprinkled with brown sugar and drizzled with cream.
• Hot applesauce topped with a pat of butter and a dash of cinnamon.
• A combo of two or more fruit juices—blend to suit your own taste.
• Orange and grapefruit sections—fresh or canned—sprinkled with pomegranate seeds.
• Melon balls with a wedge of lime.

REMEMBERED RECIPES—
TAILORED FOR TWO

Yes, you *can* cook for just two and still prepare all those wonderful dishes that stand out in your memory. Don't worry about leftovers—we've tailored the recipes so there won't be any! If a recipe does yield a leftover ingredient, often we've included alternate recipes or suggestions for its use.

This chapter includes menus for dinners, breakfasts, brunches, and luncheons. Browse through the menus—use them as a guide when you plan meals. You'll see that the menu needn't be limited in variety because the number of diners is small.

You'll also find a collection of treasured main-dish recipes and small-sized desserts—those special favorites too good to be omitted. Each recipe has been tested and retested in our Test Kitchens for ease of preparation and downright deliciousness.

You can almost smell the aroma of this Oven Swiss Steak with its golden topping of cheese. The special salad is Orange-avocado Toss—a real treat.

MEAL PLANS
JUST FOR A PAIR

⊰ MENU ⊱

Home-style Oven Dinner

Oven Swiss Steak

Baked Potatoes   *Butter*

Orange-avocado Toss

Poppy Seed Rolls   *Jelly or Jam*

Chilled Peach Halves   *Taffy Bars*

Coffee

ORANGE-AVOCADO TOSS

One hour ahead: Add ½ teaspoon shredded orange peel to ⅓ cup French dressing; set aside. Peel 1 medium avocado; slice into bottom of salad bowl. Peel 1 medium orange; remove orange sections, cutting away all white membrane. Place on top of avocado slices, covering completely. Add 2 cups bite-size pieces bibb or Boston lettuce and 1 green onion, sliced. Cover bowl with clear plastic wrap; chill in the refrigerator.

Add dressing-orange peel mixture; toss gently. Serve at once. Makes 2 servings.

OVEN SWISS STEAK

- ½ to ¾ pound boneless beef round steak, ¾-inch thick
- 2 tablespoons all-purpose flour
- ½ teaspoon salt
- 1 8-ounce can (1 cup) stewed tomatoes
- ¼ cup chopped celery
- ¼ cup chopped carrot
- 1 tablespoon chopped onion
- ¼ teaspoon Worcestershire sauce
- 2 tablespoons shredded sharp process American cheese

Cut meat into 2 portions. Mix flour and salt; pound into meat; set aside remaining flour. Brown meat in small amount of hot shortening. Place meat in small shallow baking dish. Blend remaining flour with drippings in skillet. Add remaining ingredients, except cheese, and cook, stirring constantly, till mixture boils. Pour over meat. Cover and bake in moderate oven (350°) 2 hours or till meat and vegetables are tender.

Sprinkle cheese over meat. Return to oven for few minutes. Makes 2 servings.

Baked Potatoes: Scrub and prick 2 baking potatoes; add to oven last 1¼ to 1½ hours. (For soft skins, rub potatoes first with fat.)

TAFFY BARS

- ½ cup brown sugar
- ⅓ cup shortening
- ¼ cup light molasses
- 1 egg
- 1¼ cups sifted all-purpose flour
- ½ teaspoon baking powder
- ¼ teaspoon baking soda
- ½ cup chopped walnuts

In saucepan heat and stir first 3 ingredients till shortening melts. Cool slightly. In mixer bowl beat egg. Add molasses mixture; beat till light. Sift together dry ingredients and ½ teaspoon salt; blend into mixer bowl. Stir in nuts. Spread in greased 9x9x2-inch baking pan. Bake at 350° till done, 15 to 18 minutes. Cool thoroughly; cut in bars.

BAKED POTATOES WITH CHEF'S CHEESE SAUCE

Scrub and prick 2 baking potatoes. Bake along with roast last 1¼ to 1½ hours. Serve with **Chef's Cheese Sauce:** Whip 2 tablespoons butter or margarine, softened, and ¼ cup shredded sharp process American cheese till fluffy. Add ¼ cup dairy sour cream and 1 to 2 teaspoons snipped green onion to mixture. Beat with electric mixer till blended.

MENU

Coast-to-coast Favorite

Roast Beef
Baked Potatoes　　　Chef's Cheese Sauce
or
Mashed Potatoes　　　　Perfect Gravy
Calico Skillet Salad
Hot Rolls　　　　Jam or Jelly
Ice Cream Cake Roll
Coffee

ROAST BEEF

Choose a 3½- to 4-pound sirloin tip roast.* Place fat side up on rack in shallow roasting pan; season with salt and pepper. Insert meat thermometer into center of roast. Do not add water. Roast uncovered in slow oven (325°) to desired doneness, 2 to 2¾ hours. Meat thermometer will read 140° for rare, 160° for medium, and 170° for well-done beef. Let roast stand 15 minutes to firm before carving.

*Standing rib roast (4 to 6 pounds) may be roasted similarly. No rack needed—ribs form own rack. Roast to 140° for rare, 2¼ to 2¾ hours; 160° for medium, 2¾ to 3¼ hours; 170° for well-done, 3¼ to 3½ hours.

PERFECT GRAVY

Use extra gravy with leftover meat for hot beef sandwiches at another meal—

Lift roast to hot platter. Pour drippings into glass measuring cup. Skim off fat; reserve.

For 2 cups gravy, return 3 to 4 tablespoons of the reserved fat to roasting pan or saucepan. Blend in 4 tablespoons all-purpose flour. Cook and stir over *low heat* till mixture is bubbly. Remove pan from heat. Add water or milk to meat juices to make 2 cups. Stir the liquid into pan; blend. Return to heat; cook and stir till mixture thickens and bubbles. Simmer and stir gravy 2 to 3 minutes longer.

Season to taste with salt, pepper, and monosodium glutamate. For browner gravy, add few drops kitchen bouquet sauce. Makes 2 cups.

CALICO SKILLET SALAD

  2 tablespoons butter or margarine
  1 cup coarsely shredded cabbage
 ⅓ cup bias-cut celery slices
 ⅓ cup thinly sliced carrot
  2 tablespoons slivered green
     pepper
  2 tablespoons chopped onion
 ½ teaspoon salt
     Dash pepper
  3 tablespoons light cream

Melt butter in skillet; add vegetables, salt, and pepper; cover and cook over medium heat just till vegetables are slightly tender, about 3 minutes. Add cream; heat thoroughly, stirring gently once or twice. Garnish with parsley. Serve at once. Makes 2 or 3 servings.

BEST BEEF HASH

Turn leftover beef into tasty hash—

  1 tablespoon butter or margarine
  1 cup cubed cooked roast beef
1½ cups cubed raw potato
  2 tablespoons chopped onion
 ¼ cup condensed beef broth
 ¼ teaspoon salt

Melt butter or margarine in skillet; add remaining ingredients. Mix well. Cover; cook over low heat, stirring often till potatoes are tender, about 10 minutes. Uncover and cook 5 minutes longer. Makes 2 servings.

SAVORY BEEF SUPPER

  1 cup cubed cooked roast beef
1½ cups cubed raw potato
 ½ cup condensed beef broth
  1 8-ounce can stewed tomatoes
 ½ teaspoon seasoned salt
     Dash pepper
  1 8-ounce can small white onions,
     drained

In saucepan, combine ingredients except onions. Cover and cook till potato is tender, about 20 to 25 minutes, stirring occasionally. Add onions; heat through. Makes 2 or 3 servings.

MENU

Patio Party for Two

Best Barbecued Ribs
or
Barbecue Chicken Wings (page 77)
Skillet Cabbage Slaw
Assorted Relishes
Dilly Rolls
Pineapple Crunch Cake   *Ice Cream*
Coffee

BEST BARBECUED RIBS

Cut 2 pounds pork spareribs or loin back ribs in 2 large pieces. Simmer, covered, in salted water to cover till tender, about 45 to 60 minutes; drain. Meanwhile, prepare sauce: In saucepan, combine 1/4 cup catsup, 2 tablespoons chili sauce, 1 tablespoon *each* brown sugar, butter or margarine, and chopped onion. Add 2 teaspoons prepared mustard, 1 teaspoon Worcestershire sauce, dash garlic salt, and 2 thin lemon slices. Bring mixture to boiling; remove from heat.

Grill hot ribs over medium to low coals about 10 to 15 minutes on each side, brushing often with sauce. (Or place hot ribs in shallow roasting pan; pour sauce over. Bake at 350° about 20 to 25 minutes, basting with sauce occasionally.) Makes 2 servings.

DILLY ROLLS

Split 2 hard rolls. Combine 2 tablespoons softened butter or margarine and 1/8 teaspoon dried dillweed. Spread on cut surfaces.

Wrap rolls in foil. Heat over medium to low coals about 15 minutes, turning often. Or wrap and heat in moderate oven (350°) about 15 minutes. Makes 2 servings.

Dinner right in your own backyard

←Best Barbecued Ribs cook to a turn over glowing coals. The sauce is terrific—it's seasoned just right for bold, lusty flavor.

SKILLET CABBAGE SLAW

Sour cream and apple add great flavor—

In 1-quart saucepan, fry 1 slice bacon till crisp; drain; reserve drippings; crumble bacon. Add 2 tablespoons finely chopped onion to bacon drippings and cook 2 minutes. Stir in 1 tablespoon vinegar, 1 tablespoon water, 1 1/2 teaspoons sugar, 1/4 teaspoon salt, and dash pepper. Bring just to boiling.

Add 2 cups shredded cabbage and 1 small apple, pared and finely chopped; toss to coat. Cover and cook over medium heat 5 minutes or until cabbage just wilts.

Stir in 1/4 cup dairy sour cream; top with crumbled bacon. Makes 2 or 3 servings.

PINEAPPLE CRUNCH CAKE

Cover this small-size cake with foil; next day, reheat briefly at 350°. Twice-good!

    1   8 3/4-ounce can (1 cup) crushed
          pineapple
    1/3 cup shortening
    1/2 cup granulated sugar
    1   teaspoon vanilla
    1   egg
              • • •
    1 1/4 cups sifted all-purpose flour
    1 1/2 teaspoons baking powder
    1/4 teaspoon salt
              • • •
    1/2 cup flaked coconut
    1/3 cup brown sugar
    1/3 cup chopped walnuts
    3   tablespoons butter or
          margarine, melted

Drain pineapple *thoroughly*, reserving 1/2 cup syrup. Thoroughly cream shortening, granulated sugar, and vanilla. Add egg; beat well. Sift together dry ingredients; add to creamed mixture alternately with reserved syrup, beating after each addition. Spread *half* of the batter evenly in greased and floured 8x11 1/2-inch cake pan; spoon pineapple over. Cover with remaining batter. Combine coconut, brown sugar, walnuts, and butter; sprinkle over batter. Bake in moderate oven (350°) about 35 to 40 minutes or till done. Cut in wedges. Serve warm with ice cream.

Golden biscuits, flecked with crunchy pecans and orange peel, bake atop fresh rhubarb sauce. Serve luscious Spring Rhubarb Cobbler toasty warm with cream.

⊰ MENU ⊱

Dinner's in the Oven

Cheese-baked Chicken
Crisscross Potatoes   Butter
Marinated Green Beans
Carrot Curls   Ripe Olives
Brown 'n Serve Rolls
Spring Rhubarb Cobbler or Peach Cobbler
Coffee   Milk

Oven meal strategy:

With a little advance planning, an oven meal can be a real boon to a busy homemaker:
• Plan foods that bake at same temperature.
• Remember to turn on oven to preheat *before* you begin food preparation.
• Don't crowd baking pans in oven. Heat must circulate for oven to operate properly.
• Position foods as near center of oven as possible. If you use two racks, arrange pans so they aren't directly beneath one another.
• Read oven manual carefully—be sure you know how automatic timer works. Then you can go off shopping while dinner cooks!

CHEESE-BAKED CHICKEN

    2 small chicken breasts
    1 tablespoon butter or margarine,
      melted
    ⅓ cup grated Parmesan cheese
    2 tablespoons butter or margarine

Dip chicken breasts in the 1 tablespoon melted butter or margarine, then in the Parmesan cheese. Melt remaining 2 tablespoons butter in a shallow pie plate. Place chicken breasts, skin side up, in pie plate.

Bake in a hot oven (400°) about 50 minutes or till chicken is tender. Spoon drippings over chicken once or twice during baking. Cover with foil last 15 minutes if necessary to prevent overbrowning. Makes 2 servings.

CRISSCROSS POTATOES

    1 large baking potato
    1 tablespoon butter or margarine,
      melted
      Salt
      Paprika

Scrub potato; cut in half lengthwise. Make diagonal slashes, about ⅛ inch deep in cut surface of potato, forming crisscross pattern. Brush cut surfaces with butter; season with salt. Place in small shallow pan or on piece of foil. Bake in hot oven (400°) for 40 minutes. Sprinkle potato with paprika. Bake 10 minutes more or till done. Serves 2.

MARINATED GREEN BEANS

Vegetable and salad all in one—

    ¼ cup dairy sour cream
    2 tablespoons Italian salad dressing
            • • •
    1 8-ounce can cut green beans,
      drained
    1 tomato, peeled, cubed, and drained
    2 tablespoons finely chopped onion

Thoroughly combine sour cream and Italian dressing. Add beans, tomato, and onion; mix well. Chill 3 to 4 hours before serving. Serve in lettuce cups. Makes 2 servings.

SPRING RHUBARB COBBLER

    ⅓ cup sugar
      Dash ground cinnamon
    1½ cups ½-inch pieces fresh rhubarb*
      Few drops red food coloring
    2 teaspoons butter or margarine
      Biscuit Topper

In small saucepan, combine sugar and cinnamon. Add rhubarb, ½ cup water, and food coloring. Cook and stir till mixture boils; cook 2 minutes more. Stir in butter. Pour rhubarb sauce into 2-cup baking dish or 2 individual casseroles. Spoon Biscuit Topper over *bubbling hot* sauce. Bake at 400° for 25 to 30 minutes. Serve with light cream. Serves 2.

Biscuit Topper: Sift together ⅓ cup sifted all-purpose flour, 2 tablespoons sugar, ½ teaspoon baking powder, and dash salt. Cut in 1½ tablespoons butter. Stir in 2 tablespoons milk, 2 tablespoons chopped pecans, and ¼ teaspoon shredded orange peel. Push from spoon into two dollops atop *hot* fruit.

*For frozen rhubarb: Thaw and drain ½ 16-ounce package frozen rhubarb, reserving syrup. Add enough water (about ⅔ cup) to syrup to make 1 cup. Blend 2 tablespoons sugar, 2 teaspoons cornstarch, and dash ground cinnamon in small saucepan; stir in rhubarb syrup and few drops red food coloring. Cook and stir till mixture bubbles. Add drained rhubarb and 2 teaspoons butter; heat through. Pour into 2-cup baking dish or 2 individual casseroles. Spoon Biscuit Topper (above) over *bubbling hot* sauce. Bake at 400° for 25 to 30 minutes. Serve with cream. Makes 2 servings.

PEACH COBBLER

    2 teaspoons cornstarch
    3 tablespoons brown sugar
    ¼ cup cold water
    1½ cups sliced fresh peaches
    1 tablespoon butter or margarine
    1 teaspoon lemon juice
      Biscuit Topper

Mix first 3 ingredients; add peaches. Cook and stir till bubbly. Add butter and lemon juice; pour into 2 individual casseroles. Add Biscuit Topper as for Rhubarb Cobbler (above). Bake at 400° for 25 minutes. Serves 2.

MENU

Gourmet Dinner

Cheese-stuffed Pork
or
Pork Chops Hungarian
Vegetable Rice Pilaf   Spiced Apricots
Petite Lemon Souffles
Coffee

CHEESE-STUFFED PORK

  2 double-rib pork chops
  1 3-ounce can chopped mushrooms
½ cup diced process Swiss cheese
  2 tablespoons snipped parsley
¼ cup fine dry bread crumbs
  1 beaten egg

Trim excess fat from chops; cut pocket in fat side of each chop. Drain mushrooms, reserving liquid. Combine mushrooms, cheese, parsley, and ¼ teaspoon salt; stuff into pockets. Use wooden picks to close chops; lace shut. Mix crumbs, ⅛ teaspoon salt, and dash pepper. Dip chops in egg, then crumbs; slowly brown in hot fat. Add water to reserved mushroom liquid to make ½ cup. Pour over chops; cover; simmer 1 hour or till tender. Serves 2.

VEGETABLE RICE PILAF

⅓ cup uncooked long-grain rice
  1 tablespoon finely chopped onion
  2 tablespoons butter or margarine
  1 chicken bouillon cube
  1 8-ounce can mixed vegetables

Cook rice and onion in butter 5 to 10 minutes or till lightly browned, stirring frequently. Add 1 cup water, bouillon cube, and ¼ teaspoon salt. Bring to boil, stirring to dissolve bouillon cube. Reduce heat; cover and cook slowly about 20 minutes or till liquid is absorbed and rice is fluffy. Drain vegetables and stir in; heat through. Serves 2.

PETITE LEMON SOUFFLES

  2 slightly beaten egg yolks
  2 tablespoons butter or margarine, softened
  2 tablespoons sugar
    Dash salt
¼ teaspoon grated lemon peel
  2 tablespoons lemon juice
    • • •
  2 egg whites
  2 tablespoons sugar

Combine the first 6 ingredients in small heavy saucepan. Cook over low heat, stirring constantly, till thick. Remove from heat and beat well, about 2 minutes; set aside.

Beat egg whites to soft peaks. Gradually add 2 tablespoons sugar, beating to stiff peaks. Fold egg yolk mixture into whites till blended. Spoon into 2 individual souffle dishes or two 10-ounce glass baking dishes.

Place souffle dishes in shallow baking dish; pour boiling water around dishes to depth of ½ inch. Bake in a moderate oven (350°) about 35 minutes or till tops spring back when lightly touched in center. Sprinkle tops lightly with sifted confectioners' sugar. Serve immediately. Makes 2 servings.

PORK CHOPS HUNGARIAN

  2 loin pork chops, ¾-inch thick
  1 small onion, thinly sliced
¼ teaspoon caraway seed
¼ teaspoon salt
¼ teaspoon paprika
⅛ teaspoon dried dillweed
    Dash garlic powder
½ cup water
    • • •
⅓ cup dairy sour cream

Trim fat from chops. Brown chops in small amount of hot shortening in 8-inch skillet; drain off excess fat. Combine onion, caraway seed, salt, paprika, dillweed, garlic powder, and water; add to skillet. Cover and cook over medium heat for 45 to 60 minutes or till pork chops are tender. Transfer chops to warm platter. Stir sour cream into meat drippings in skillet. Heat through but do not boil. Spoon sauce over chops. Makes 2 servings.

Weekend Brunch

Quick Cranberry Ice
Saucy Ham 'n Eggs in
Caraway Puffs
Cheese-topped Lettuce
Peanut Butter Brownies (page 70)
Coffee

Caraway Puffs are flavorful "containers" for Saucy Ham 'n Eggs. Or, make appetizer-size puffs; fill with a ham salad mixture.

SAUCY HAM 'N EGGS IN CARAWAY PUFFS

Puffs:
- 2 tablespoons butter or margarine
- ¼ cup sifted all-purpose flour
- 1 egg
- ½ teaspoon caraway seed

Melt the butter in ¼ cup boiling water. Add the flour and dash salt and stir vigorously. Cook and stir till mixture forms a ball that doesn't separate. Remove from heat and cool slightly. Add the egg, beating vigorously till mixture is smooth. Stir in caraway seed.

Drop dough in two portions, 3 inches apart, on greased baking sheet. Bake in very hot oven (450°) for 15 minutes. Reduce heat to 325°; bake 25 minutes more. Remove puffs from oven; cool slightly. Slice off top and remove moist membrane in each puff.

Filling:
- 1½ tablespoons butter or margarine
- 1½ tablespoons all-purpose flour
- 1 cup milk
- ½ cup cubed cooked ham
- 2 hard-cooked eggs, sliced
- 1 teaspoon chopped canned pimiento
- 2 tablespoons chopped green pepper

Melt butter in saucepan over low heat; blend in flour, ¼ teaspoon salt, and dash pepper. Add milk all at once. Cook and stir till mixture thickens and bubbles. Add remaining ingredients; heat through. Spoon mixture into caraway puffs; serve immediately. Serves 2.

QUICK CRANBERRY ICE

- 1 8-ounce can jellied cranberry sauce
- 1 or 2 drops red food coloring
- ½ cup lemon-lime carbonated beverage

Turn cranberry sauce and food coloring into mixer bowl; beat till smooth. Slowly pour in lemon-lime beverage. Mix gently. Pour into small refrigerator tray; cover; freeze till firm.

Remove from freezer; break mixture into chunks. Turn into chilled mixer bowl; beat till fluffy. Return to tray; cover; freeze. Spoon into sherbet glasses. Makes 4 servings.

CHEESE-TOPPED LETTUCE

Thoroughly chill 2 ounces blue cheese in freezer 20 to 30 minutes. Cut 2 crosswise slices from head of lettuce. Place lettuce slices on salad plates. Spoon oil and vinegar salad dressing over each. Shred a generous fluff of blue cheese over each. Serves 2.

HAM SALAD FRUIT BOATS

    1 small pineapple, chilled
    1 cup cubed cooked ham
    ½ cup sliced celery
    1 tablespoon chopped green pepper
    ¼ cup mayonnaise or salad dressing
    ½ teaspoon prepared mustard

Cut pineapple in half lengthwise. Remove hard core. Cut around edge of fruit, leaving a rim about ½-inch thick. Cut loosened fruit crosswise; remove and dice. Combine 1 cup of the diced pineapple with ham, celery, and green pepper. (Reserve remaining pineapple for another meal.) Blend mayonnaise and mustard; add to ham mixture. Toss to coat ingredients. Spoon into pineapple boats. Serves 2.

CHICKEN SALAD ELEGANTE

    1 cup diced cooked chicken
    1 tablespoon clear French salad
       dressing with spices and herbs
    ½ cup halved seedless green grapes
    ¼ cup chopped celery
    2 tablespoons slivered almonds,
       toasted
    ⅓ cup mayonnaise or salad dressing
    ½ teaspoon lemon juice

Mix chicken and French dressing; chill 1 hour. Add grapes, celery, and nuts. Combine mayonnaise, lemon juice, dash salt, and dash pepper; toss with salad. Chill. Serve in crisp lettuce cups. Makes 2 servings.

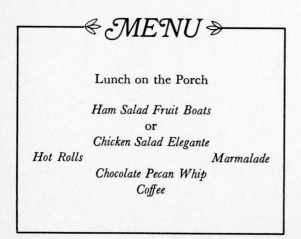

⇚ *MENU* ⇛

Lunch on the Porch

Ham Salad Fruit Boats
or
Chicken Salad Elegante
Hot Rolls   *Marmalade*
Chocolate Pecan Whip
Coffee

CHOCOLATE PECAN WHIP

    1 teaspoon unflavored gelatin
    2 tablespoons sugar
       Dash salt
       • • •
    1 egg yolk
    ¾ cup milk
    ½ teaspoon vanilla
       • • •
    1 egg white
    2 tablespoons sugar
    ¼ cup whipping cream, whipped
    2 tablespoons semisweet chocolate
       pieces, chopped
    2 tablespoons chopped pecans

In saucepan, thoroughly mix gelatin, 2 tablespoons sugar, and salt. Beat together egg yolk and milk; stir into gelatin mixture. Cook and stir over low heat till slightly thickened. Add vanilla; chill till partially set.

    Beat egg white to soft peaks. Gradually add 2 tablespoons sugar, beating to stiff peaks; fold into gelatin mixture. Fold in whipped cream, chopped chocolate, and pecans. Spoon into sherbets. Chill at least 2 hours. Garnish with additional pecans just before serving. Makes 2 or 3 servings.

Nice to serve:

  • Lunch on brightly colored trays—to be toted to the porch or wherever you wish.

  • Salad-filled pineapple boats in a bed of crushed ice to bring down the temperature on a warm summer day.

  • Hot rolls nestled in individual napkin-lined baskets—one for each tray so they'll stay toasty warm all through lunch.

  • Dessert right on the luncheon tray (when it's one that will wait well) so you can relax and won't have to dash back to the kitchen for last minute fuss at dessert time.

  • Coffee from an electric coffee maker plugged in on the porch.

Leisurely summertime luncheon

Ham Salad Fruit Boats feature ham tossed → with succulent cubes of fresh pineapple, then served in shells—Island-style.

MENU

Sunday Breakfast

Broiled Grapefruit
Soft-cooked Eggs   *Bacon* or *Ham*
Coffee Cake or *Toast*
Coffee

BROILED GRAPEFRUIT

Have 1 grapefruit at room temperature. Cut in half; then cut a thin slice from the bottom of each half to balance fruit. Cut around every section, close to membrane—fruit should be completely loosened from shell. Remove core from each half; dot with butter.

Combine 1 tablespoon sugar and ¼ teaspoon ground cinnamon; sprinkle over grapefruit. Place on broiler rack or in shallow baking pan. Broil 4 inches from heat about 8 minutes or till heated through and bubbling. Garnish with maraschino cherries. Serves 2.

SOFT-COOKED EGGS

Place eggs in saucepan and cover with cold water (at least 1 inch above eggs); rapidly bring to boiling. Cover pan tightly and remove from heat. Start timing now—leave in water 2 to 4 minutes depending upon individual taste. Promptly cool eggs in cold water a few seconds to stop cooking.

Also nice for breakfast:

• Sliced bananas in orange juice, sprinkled with confectioners' sugar.
• Toasted English muffins with marmalade —keep muffins on hand in freezer.
• Fresh fruit and ice cream atop cereal.
• Butter-grilled or broiled thick tomato slices seasoned with dillweed.
• Cinnamon stick stirrers swirled in mugs of steaming coffee or cocoa.
• Equal amounts of chilled pineapple and tomato juices in glasses with lemon trim. Pour pineapple juice in glass before *slowly* pouring tomato juice down side of glass.

FRENCH TOAST FOR TWO

Combine 1 slightly beaten egg, ½ cup milk, dash ground nutmeg, and dash salt. Dip 4 slices day-old bread in mixture. Brown on both sides in 2 tablespoons hot butter or margarine till golden. Serve hot with syrup.

ORANGE FRENCH TOAST

Combine 1 slightly beaten egg, ⅓ cup orange juice, dash ground cinnamon, and dash salt. Dip 4 slices day-old bread in mixture. Brown on both sides in 2 tablespoons hot butter or margarine till golden. Serve hot with confectioners' sugar.

HASHED BROWN POTATOES

  2 small baking potatoes
  1 tablespoon finely chopped onion
 ¼ teaspoon salt
  2 tablespoons butter or margarine

Boil potatoes in jackets; chill. Peel and coarsely shred (1½ cups). Add onion, salt, and dash pepper. Melt butter in 8-inch skillet. Pat potatoes into pan, leaving ½-inch space around edge. Brown about 9 minutes. Reduce heat if necessary; turn. Brown about 5 minutes longer or till golden. Serves 2.

ORANGE TOASTIES

  2 tablespoons butter, softened
  2 tablespoons orange marmalade
    Dash ground nutmeg
  4 slices French bread, ½ inch thick
    Flaked coconut

Combine butter, marmalade, and nutmeg. Spread mixture on French bread. Place on baking sheet. Sprinkle with coconut. Bake at 400° for 5 minutes or till coconut is toasted.

A delightful way to greet the day

Serve Soft-cooked Eggs in pretty egg cups. →
With egg scissors or knife, snip off top of egg, then spoon into warm golden center.

ROUND-UP OF TREASURED RECIPES

FRANKFURTER PIZZA

Sift 1 cup sifted all-purpose flour, 1½ teaspoons baking powder, and ¼ teaspoon salt. Add ½ teaspoon *dry* garlic salad dressing mix. Cut in 2 tablespoons shortening. Add ⅓ cup milk. Stir just till moistened. Knead dough on lightly floured surface 10 strokes. Roll to 10-inch circle; pat in bottom of greased 9-inch pie plate, building up ½-inch edge.

Combine ⅓ cup pizza-flavored catsup, 1 tablespoon salad oil, and dash dried oregano, crushed; spread on crust. Top with 3 frankfurters, cut in ½-inch slices, and ¼ cup ripe olives, sliced; sprinkle with ½ cup shredded sharp process American cheese. Bake at 450° for 12 to 15 minutes. Serves 2.

SAUSAGE PIZZA BAKE

½ pound bulk pork sausage
¼ cup chopped green pepper
2 tablespoons chopped onion
¼ teaspoon dried oregano, crushed
1 8-ounce can tomato sauce
½ cup elbow macaroni, cooked
¼ cup grated Parmesan cheese

Brown sausage; pour off excess fat. Add green pepper, onion, oregano, and dash pepper. Stir in tomato sauce and ½ cup water. Simmer 5 minutes. Drain macaroni; mix into sausage with 2 *tablespoons* cheese. Turn into 1-quart casserole. Sprinkle remaining cheese atop. Cover; bake at 350° about 25 minutes. Serves 2.

Frankfurter Pizza is flavorful and easy on the budget. Next time make it with pepperoni or another cheese. Add onions, mushrooms, or green pepper if you like.

PERFECT FRIED CHICKEN

- ⅓ cup all-purpose flour
- 1 teaspoon salt
- 1 teaspoon paprika
- ¼ teaspoon pepper
- 1 2- to 2½-pound ready-to-cook broiler-fryer chicken, cut up

Combine flour and seasonings in paper or plastic bag; add 2 or 3 pieces of chicken at a time and shake. Heat shortening (¼ inch deep in skillet) till a drop of water sizzles.

Brown meaty pieces first; then add others (don't crowd). Turn pieces once. When lightly browned, 15 to 20 minutes, reduce heat; cover tightly. (If cover isn't tight, add 1 tablespoon water.) Cook till tender, 30 to 40 minutes. Uncover last 10 minutes. Makes 2 servings.

Note: For extra crustiness, add ½ cup fine dry bread crumbs to flour for the coating.

CHILI FOR TWO

- ¼ pound ground beef
- 1 8-ounce can kidney beans, drained
- 1 16-ounce can tomatoes, cut up
- ¼ teaspoon salt
- ½ teaspoon chili powder
- 2 tablespoons instant minced onion

Brown meat; add remaining ingredients; mix well. Bring to boil; cover and simmer for 20 minutes, stirring occasionally. Serves 2.

CHICKEN CHEESE SOUP

- ⅓ cup shredded carrot
- 2 tablespoons chopped onion
- 2 tablespoons butter or margarine
- 1 10½-ounce can condensed cream of chicken soup
- ½ teaspoon Worcestershire sauce
- 2 ounces sharp process American cheese, shredded (½ cup)

Cook carrot and onion in butter till almost tender. Stir in soup. Gradually add 1 cup water and the Worcestershire, mixing till smooth. Heat to boiling; add cheese; stir till melted. Garnish with croutons. Serves 2.

DILLED LAMB STEW

- 1 pound boneless lamb, cut in ¾-inch cubes (2 cups)
- ½ teaspoon salt
- ¼ teaspoon dried dillweed
- 1 cup water
- 1 cup sliced carrot
- ½ cup sliced celery
- 1 tablespoon all-purpose flour
- ½ cup cold water
- ½ cup dairy sour cream

Trim any fat from lamb; rub skillet with fat; discard. Brown lamb in skillet. Sprinkle with salt and dillweed; add the 1 cup water. Cover; simmer about 35 minutes, or till almost tender.

Add carrot and celery; cook 15 minutes more. Blend flour with the ½ cup water; stir into stew. Cook till mixture thickens and boils. Stir in sour cream; heat through. Serves 2 or 3.

CHICKEN FRICASSEE WITH LEMON DUMPLINGS

- 4 chicken drumsticks
- 1 cup water
- ¼ cup diced celery
- 1 tablespoon chopped onion
- 1 teaspoon chicken-flavored gravy base
- ½ teaspoon salt
  Dash pepper
- 3 tablespoons all-purpose flour
- ½ 10-ounce package (about 1 cup) frozen mixed vegetables
  Lemon Dumplings

In 2-quart saucepan, simmer drumsticks with the 1 cup water, the celery, onion, gravy base, salt, and pepper for 20 minutes or till chicken is tender. Blend flour and ½ cup cold water; stir into broth. Cook and stir over medium heat, till gravy thickens. Stir in vegetables.

Meanwhile, for *Lemon Dumplings:* Combine ⅓ cup all-purpose flour, ½ teaspoon baking powder, and ¼ teaspoon salt. Combine ¼ cup milk, ½ teaspoon snipped parsley, ¼ teaspoon grated lemon peel, and ½ teaspoon lemon juice. Add to dry ingredients; stir just till moistened. Drop batter in mounds atop *bubbling hot* chicken mixture. Cover; simmer 20 minutes. Makes 2 servings.

SWEET POTATO CASSEROLE

Team up with Canadian-style bacon glazed with a little maple syrup—

1 8-ounce can sweet potatoes,
  drained
2 tablespoons milk
2 tablespoons butter or margarine,
  melted

• • •

2 tablespoons raisins
2 tablespoons orange marmalade
  Dash salt
  Dash ground cinnamon
  Dash ground nutmeg
½ cup miniature marshmallows

Mash potatoes; stir in milk and melted butter. Add raisins, orange marmalade, salt, cinnamon, and nutmeg. Mix well. Place in a 2-cup casserole. Bake in a moderate oven (350°) for 25 minutes. Top with marshmallows. Return to oven for 8 to 10 minutes or till marshmallows are lightly browned. Makes 2 servings.

STUFFED PEPPERS

All-time ground beef favorite—

1 large or 2 small green peppers
½ pound ground beef
¼ cup uncooked packaged precooked
  rice
½ teaspoon salt
  Dash pepper
½ teaspoon Worcestershire sauce
1 tablespoon chopped onion
1 egg
1 8-ounce can tomato sauce

Halve large pepper or cut tops off small ones; remove seeds and membranes. Precook peppers in boiling salted water about 5 minutes; drain. Combine ground beef, rice, salt, pepper, Worcestershire sauce, onion, egg, and ¼ *cup* of the tomato sauce; mix thoroughly.

Stuff peppers and stand upright in very small casserole. Pour remaining tomato sauce over stuffed peppers. Cover and bake in a moderate oven (350°) for 45 to 50 minutes or till done. Baste peppers with sauce 2 or 3 times during baking. Makes 2 servings.

LAMB CHOP RICE BAKE

Brown two ½-inch thick shoulder lamb chops in small amount of hot shortening; season with salt and pepper. In small baking dish, combine ½ cup uncooked long-grain rice, ⅓ cup orange juice, and one 10½-ounce can condensed chicken with rice soup. Arrange chops on top. Cover and bake in a moderate oven (350°) for 30 minutes.

Mix 1 tablespoon brown sugar, 1 teaspoon prepared mustard, and ½ teaspoon Worcestershire sauce. Uncover chops and brush with mixture. Bake 25 minutes longer. Serves 2.

FRENCH VEAL CHOPS

2 veal rib chops
1 cup chopped onion
1 tablespoon butter or margarine
¼ cup dry white wine
1 cup soft bread crumbs
2 tablespoons grated Parmesan
  cheese
1 tablespoon butter, melted

Sprinkle chops with ½ teaspoon salt and dash pepper; brown in 1 tablespoon salad oil in small skillet. Place chopped onion in 9-inch pie plate; dot with 1 tablespoon butter. Place chops on onion; pour wine over. Combine crumbs, cheese, and melted butter; sprinkle atop. Bake at 350° for 1 hour. Serves 2.

CREAMED CHICKEN LIVERS

4 slices bacon
2 tablespoons all-purpose flour
8 ounces chicken livers
1 tablespoon chopped onion
1 10½-ounce can condensed cream of
  mushroom soup
1 cup hot cooked rice

Fry bacon till crisp; remove from skillet and drain, reserving drippings. Combine flour and dash pepper; coat livers. Brown livers and onion in 2 tablespoons bacon drippings. Cover and cook over low heat for 8 to 10 minutes.

Blend soup with ¼ cup water; stir into livers; heat through. To serve, spoon over hot cooked rice; top with bacon strips. Serves 2.

BACON-LIVER BAKE

   3 slices bacon
   2 tablespoons all-purpose flour
  ½ teaspoon salt
     Dash pepper
  ½ pound calves liver, cut in pieces
   1 cup milk
 1½ teaspoons instant minced onion
   2 tablespoons fine dry bread crumbs
     or ½ cup soft bread crumbs
   1 teaspoon butter, melted

Fry bacon in skillet till crisp; remove, reserving drippings. Combine flour, salt, and pepper. Dip liver in flour mixture (reserve extra flour); brown in bacon drippings. Remove liver to 2-cup casserole. Blend remaining flour with drippings in skillet till smooth. Add milk; stir in onion. Cook and stir till thickened and bubbly. Pour sauce over liver; crumble bacon over all. Combine crumbs and melted butter; sprinkle atop casserole. Bake at 350° about 45 minutes. Makes 2 servings.

Favorite Pancakes are light and tender. For a treat, drop a few well-drained blueberries onto each pancake just before turning.

FRENCH FRIED SHRIMP

 ¾ pound large raw shrimp in shells
 ½ cup sifted all-purpose flour
 ¼ teaspoon sugar
 ¼ teaspoon salt
    Dash curry powder
 1 egg white
 ½ cup water
 1 tablespoon salad oil

Peel shells from shrimp, leaving tails. Slit along back; remove veins. Flatten shimp; pat dry. Combine dry ingredients; add egg white, water, and salad oil; beat well. Dip shrimp in batter; fry in deep hot fat (375°) till golden brown, about 5 minutes. Remove and drain on paper towels. Serve immediately with cocktail or tartar sauce. Makes 2 servings.

ONION-CHEDDAR SOUP

 ½ cup chopped onion
 2 tablespoons butter or margarine
 2 tablespoons all-purpose flour
 ¼ teaspoon salt
    Dash pepper
 2 cups milk
 4 ounces sharp process
    American cheese, shredded (1 cup)

Cook onion in butter till tender but not brown. Blend in flour, salt, and pepper. Add milk all at once. Bring to boiling, stirring constantly. Remove from heat. Add cheese; stir till melted. Garnish with paprika and snipped chives. Makes 2 or 3 servings.

FAVORITE PANCAKES

 ⅔ cup sifted all-purpose flour
 1½ teaspoons baking powder
 1½ teaspoons sugar
 ¼ teaspoon salt
 1 beaten egg
 ½ cup milk
 1 tablespoon salad oil

Sift together dry ingredients. Combine egg, milk, and oil; add to dry ingredients, stirring just till moistened. Bake on hot, lightly greased griddle. Makes four 4-inch pancakes.

SMALL-SIZED DESSERTS

CHOCOLATE DESSERT DUET

¼ cup semisweet chocolate pieces
2⅔ cups miniature marshmallows
2 tablespoons water
Dash salt
1 egg
¼ teaspoon vanilla
½ cup whipping cream, whipped
2 tablespoons slivered almonds, toasted

Combine chocolate, marshmallows, water, and salt in top of double boiler. Cook and stir over hot water till completely melted. Separate egg. Beat egg yolk slightly. Stir in small amount of chocolate mixture; return to hot mixture. Cook and stir 2 minutes. Remove from heat; add vanilla. Beat smooth; cool.

Beat egg white till stiff peaks form. Fold into chocolate mixture. Fold in whipped cream. Spoon mixture into 2 sherbets and 2 foil bake cups. Top with toasted slivered almonds. Chill sherbets and freeze bake cups. Makes 2 chilled and 2 frozen desserts.

FRUIT WITH DUMPLINGS

1 8-ounce can fruit cocktail
1 tablespoon sugar
1 teaspoon butter or margarine
1 teaspoon lemon juice
½ cup sifted all-purpose flour
2 tablespoons sugar
1 teaspoon baking powder
¼ teaspoon salt
¼ cup milk
1 teaspoon salad oil
Ground cinnamon or nutmeg

Combine first 4 ingredients in saucepan. Bring to boil. In small bowl, sift together dry ingredients. Stir in milk and oil. Drop in 2 portions onto *boiling hot* fruit. Sprinkle lightly with cinnamon or nutmeg. Cover; cook over medium heat for 10 to 12 minutes. Serve with light cream. Makes 2 servings.

BAKED PEARS ELEGANTE

2 medium fresh Bartlett pears
½ cup port wine
¼ cup sugar
1½ inches stick cinnamon
3 whole cloves
Dash salt
3 thin lemon slices

Pare, halve, and core pears; place in 1-quart baking dish. In a saucepan, combine remaining ingredients; add a few drops red food coloring if desired. Bring to boiling; pour over pears. Bake, covered, at 350° for 20 minutes. Uncover and bake 10 minutes or till tender, basting once or twice. Serve hot, or chill and top with whipped cream. Serves 2.

MAPLE SHORTBREAD BARS

1¼ cups sifted all-purpose flour
¼ cup sugar
½ cup butter or margarine
⅔ cup maple-blended syrup
1⅓ cups flaked coconut

Sift together flour and sugar. Cut in butter till mixture resembles fine crumbs. Press into an 8x8x2-inch baking pan. Bake in moderate oven (375°) for 15 to 20 minutes. Combine syrup, coconut, and ¼ teaspoon salt in small saucepan. Cook till coconut absorbs most of syrup, about 8 minutes. Spread over warm crumbs; bake 10 minutes. Cut in bars.

FRUIT AND RICE COMPOTE

Cook ¼ cup long-grain rice with 1½ cups water till tender; drain. Drain one 8¾-ounce can apricot halves reserving 2 tablespoons syrup. Combine reserved syrup, cooked rice, 3 tablespoons sweet orange marmalade, and 1 tablespoon lemon juice. Spoon into 2-cup baking dish; top with apricots. Bake at 375° for 20 minutes. Makes 2 servings.

PRUNE SPICE CAKE

    1 cup sifted all-purpose flour
    ⅔ cup sugar
    1 teaspoon baking powder
    ¼ teaspoon soda
    ¼ teaspoon ground cinnamon
    ¼ teaspoon ground nutmeg
    ¼ cup shortening
    ½ cup prune juice
    1 egg
    ½ teaspoon vanilla
      Prune Butter Frosting

Sift together flour, sugar, baking powder, soda, ¼ teaspoon salt, and spices into mixer bowl. Add shortening, *half* the prune juice, and egg. Beat 2 minutes with electric mixer. Add remaining prune juice and vanilla. Beat 2 minutes. Pour into well-greased and lightly floured 8x8x2-inch baking pan. Bake at 350° for 25 to 30 minutes, or till done. Cool.

Frost with *Prune Butter Frosting:* Cream 3 tablespoons butter; gradually add 1½ cups sifted confectioners' sugar and dash salt, blending well. Add enough prune juice (about 1 tablespoon) for spreading consistency.

CHOCOLATE FUDGE CAKE

    ⅓ cup shortening
    1 cup sugar
    ½ teaspoon vanilla
    2 squares (2 ounces) unsweetened
      chocolate, melted and cooled
    1 egg
    1¼ cups sifted all-purpose flour
    ½ teaspoon soda
    ½ teaspoon salt
    ½ cup semisweet chocolate pieces
    9 walnut halves

Cream shortening and sugar till light and fluffy. Blend in vanilla and cooled chocolate. Add egg, beating well. Sift together flour, soda, and salt; add to creamed mixture alternately with ¾ cup water, beating after each addition. Spread batter in greased and lightly floured 9x9x2-inch baking pan. Sprinkle with chocolate pieces. Arrange walnut halves over top. Bake in moderate oven (350°) about 30 minutes or till cake springs back when touched in center. Cool in pan.

Cake baking has never been this easy! Chocolate Fudge Cake has its own built-in chocolate and nut frosting baked on top.

Quick ice cream ideas:

• Top scoops of lemon sherbet with frozen red raspberries, partially thawed.
• Fill chilled canned peach halves with vanilla ice cream. Spoon raspberry topping over.
• Sandwich peppermint ice cream between slices of chocolate cake or pound cake.

PASTRY FOR 4-INCH PIES

½ cup sifted all-purpose flour
¼ teaspoon salt
3 tablespoons shortening
1 to 1½ tablespoons cold water

To make pastry shell, sift together flour and salt; cut in shortening till mixture resembles coarse crumbs. Sprinkle 1 *tablespoon* of the water over. Gently toss with fork and push moistened part to one side. Repeat with remaining ½ tablespoon water if needed.

Gather up mixture with fingers; form into two balls. On lightly floured surface, flatten balls slightly; roll to 7-inch rounds. If edges split, pinch together. Roll up pastry on rolling pin; unroll over two 4¼-inch tart pans, fitting loosely onto bottom and sides. Trim ½ inch beyond edge. Turn under; flute.

For baked shell, prick bottom and sides with fork. Bake in very hot oven (450°) for 10 to 12 minutes or till golden brown.

For unbaked shell, do not prick. Add filling; bake as directed in pie recipe.

To make pastry for 2-crust pie, use ¾ cup flour, ¼ teaspoon salt, ¼ cup shortening, and 2 to 2½ tablespoons cold water.

Note: To make two single-crust 4¼-inch pies from pie crust mix, use ½ stick pie crust mix and 1 tablespoon water *or* ⅔ cup crumbly pie crust mix and 1 to 1½ tablespoons water. Prepare according to package directions.

CRUMB-TOP APPLE PIE

¼ cup sugar
¼ teaspoon ground cinnamon
1½ cups cored, pared, sliced, tart apples
2 4¼-inch *unbaked* pastry shells
1 tablespoon sugar
2 tablespoons all-purpose flour
1 tablespoon butter or margarine

Combine the ¼ cup sugar and the cinnamon; mix with apples; arrange in pastry shells. Combine the 1 tablespoon sugar and the flour. Cut in butter till crumbly; sprinkle over apples. Bake in hot oven (400°) for 35 to 40 minutes or till apples are tender and topping browned. Cool; serve with ice cream, if desired. Makes 2 servings.

VANILLA CREAM PIE

¼ cup sugar
1 tablespoon cornstarch
Dash salt
⅔ cup milk
1 slightly beaten egg yolk
1 tablespoon butter or margarine
¼ teaspoon vanilla
2 4¼-inch *baked* pastry shells
Meringue

In saucepan, combine sugar, cornstarch, and salt; gradually stir in milk. Cook and stir till mixture thickens and boils; cook and stir 1 minute longer. Remove from heat. Stir small amount of hot mixture into egg yolk. Return to hot mixture; cook 2 minutes, stirring constantly. Remove from heat; add butter and vanilla. Pour into pastry shells.

For *Meringue:* Beat 1 egg white with dash cream of tartar and ¼ teaspoon vanilla to soft peaks. Gradually add 2 tablespoons sugar, beating to stiff peaks. Spread atop pies, sealing to edges of pastry. Bake in moderate oven (350°) for 10 to 12 minutes or till meringue is golden. Cool. Makes 2 servings.

Chocolate Cream Pie: Follow recipe for Vanilla Cream Pie, increasing sugar to ⅓ cup in filling. Add ½ square (½ ounce) unsweetened chocolate, chopped, with the milk.

Butterscotch Cream Pie: Follow recipe for Vanilla Cream Pie, substituting light brown sugar for the granulated sugar in filling.

PECAN PIE

1 egg
¼ cup sugar
Dash salt
⅓ cup dark corn syrup
2 tablespoons butter or margarine, melted
⅓ cup pecan halves
2 4¼-inch *unbaked* pastry shells

Beat egg thoroughly with sugar, salt, corn syrup, and butter; add pecans. Pour into pastry shells. Bake at 350° for 40 to 45 minutes or till knife inserted between center and edge comes out clean. Cool. Serves 2.

LEMON SOUR CREAM PIE

⅓ cup sugar
1 tablespoon cornstarch
Dash salt
⅓ cup milk
1 slightly beaten egg yolk
1 tablespoon butter or margarine
¼ teaspoon shredded lemon peel
4 teaspoons lemon juice
⅓ cup dairy sour cream
2 4¼-inch *baked* pastry shells

• • •

1 egg white
Dash cream of tartar
¼ teaspoon vanilla
2 tablespoons sugar

In saucepan, combine sugar, cornstarch, and salt; stir in milk. Cook and stir over medium-high heat till thickened and bubbly; cook and stir 1 minute more. Blend small amount of hot mixture into egg yolk; return to hot mixture. Cook 2 minutes, stirring constantly.

Remove from heat; add butter, lemon peel, and juice. Cover; cool to room temperature. Fold in sour cream; spoon into pastry shells.

Beat egg white with cream of tartar and vanilla to soft peaks. Gradually add sugar, beating to stiff peaks. Spread meringue atop pies, sealing to edge of pastry. Bake in moderate oven (350°) for 10 to 12 minutes or till meringue is golden brown. Makes 2 servings.

ORANGE TAPIOCA FLUFF

2 tablespoons quick-cooking tapioca
2 tablespoons sugar
Dash salt
1 egg yolk
1 cup orange juice
1 egg white
2 tablespoons sugar

In 1½-quart saucepan, combine tapioca, 2 tablespoons sugar, and dash salt. Blend in egg yolk and orange juice; let stand 5 minutes. Bring to boil over medium heat, stirring often. Remove from heat. Beat egg white till soft peaks form; gradually add 2 tablespoons sugar, beating till stiff peaks form. Fold orange mixture into egg white mixture; cool. Spoon into sherbet glasses; chill. Makes 2 or 3 servings.

CRANBERRY DUMPLINGS

For a more tart and tangy dessert, reduce the sugar cooked with cranberries—

1 cup fresh cranberries
¾ cup sugar
½ cup water
¼ cup orange juice
⅓ cup sifted all-purpose flour
½ teaspoon baking powder
Dash salt
2 tablespoons sugar
2 tablespoons flaked coconut
1 egg yolk
1 tablespoon milk
1 tablespoon butter or margarine, melted

In 2-quart saucepan, combine cranberries, the ¾ cup sugar, the water, and orange juice; cover and simmer 10 minutes. Sift together flour, baking powder, salt, and the 2 tablespoons sugar; stir in the coconut. Combine egg yolk, milk, and butter or margarine; stir into flour mixture just till blended.

Drop in 2 portions onto *boiling hot* cranberry mixture. Simmer, tightly covered, 20 minutes. Serve with light cream. Serves 2.

SPECIAL BAKED APPLES

2 large baking apples
¼ cup coarsely snipped dates *or*
   ¼ cup raisins
1 tablespoon coarsely chopped walnuts
¼ teaspoon grated orange peel
⅓ cup brown sugar
⅓ cup water
1 tablespoon butter or margarine
¼ teaspoon ground cinnamon
¼ teaspoon ground nutmeg

Core apples; pare top quarter of each. Combine dates, walnuts, and orange peel. Place apples in a loaf pan or two 10-ounce glass baking dishes. Fill centers with date mixture.

In saucepan, combine remaining ingredients. Bring to boil; pour around apples. Bake, uncovered, in moderate oven (350°) for 1 to 1¼ hours or till apples are done. Baste occasionally with sauce. Makes 2 servings.

SHOP AND SERVE SPECIALS

Even when cooking for only two, it's easy to run short on time—so we've provided some quick and easy recipes for you. Check this chapter, then stock your pantry so you'll be able to serve on the spur of the moment.

You'll find magic main dishes that take advantage of canned foods and other convenience items. In most cases, it pays to buy the small-sized items called for in these recipes—a big can or package is a real money saver only if you have a use for all of it.

Sandwiches are a wonderful way to provide hearty eating for two without leftovers. We've included some unique fillings for the traditional two-slice sandwich as well as several tasty open-facers and knife-and-fork type sandwiches. This chapter also gives an assortment of sweet tooth "goodies"—fruit desserts, quick pies, those half-cookie half-candy confections—that can be made in the wink of an eye.

Get out the chopsticks for Oriental Skillet Supper. Prepare this delicious beef-tomato-pepper mixture in about 10 minutes, then serve it on Ginger Rice.

MAIN DISHES LIKE MAGIC

SNAPPERONI FRANKS

    4 frankfurters
    1 9-ounce can pork and beans
       in tomato sauce
    2 tablespoons diced pepperoni
    1 tablespoon catsup
    2 teaspoons pickle relish
    2 frankfurter buns, split

Place franks in boiling water; simmer, covered, 5 to 8 minutes. Meanwhile, mash beans slightly with fork. Combine beans, pepperoni, catsup, and pickle relish; cook and stir till heated through. Toast buns. Place a frank on each bun half; spoon bean mixture over. Serves 2.

GLAZED APPLES 'N FRANKS

    1 tablespoon butter or margarine
    2 teaspoons prepared mustard
    ¼ cup light corn syrup
    4 frankfurters
    2 tart apples, cored, pared,
       and quartered

In skillet, melt butter; blend in mustard and corn syrup. Add franks and apples. Cover; cook over low heat 10 to 15 minutes or till apples are tender, turning once. Serve over rice, if desired. Pass pan juices. Serves 2.

CHEESEBURGER CHOWDER

    ¼ pound ground beef
    ¼ cup chopped onion
    2 tablespoons chopped green pepper
    1 11-ounce can condensed Cheddar
       cheese soup
    1 soup can milk (1¼ cups)
       Dash Worcestershire sauce

In small skillet or saucepan, cook beef, onion, and green pepper till meat is lightly browned. Blend in remaining ingredients; simmer about 5 minutes. Makes 2 servings.

ORIENTAL SKILLET SUPPER

    ½ cup green pepper strips
    ⅓ cup bias-cut celery slices
    1 tablespoon salad oil
    1 large or 2 small minute steaks,
       cut in ¼-inch strips
    ⅓ cup cold water
    1 tablespoon soy sauce
    2 teaspoons cornstarch
    ½ teaspoon sugar
    ¼ teaspoon salt
    1 medium tomato, peeled and cut
       in wedges
    1 cup hot cooked rice
    ¼ teaspoon ground ginger

In heavy skillet, quickly cook green pepper and celery in oil till crisp-tender. Remove and set aside. Add meat to hot skillet; brown quickly. Combine water, soy, cornstarch, sugar, and salt; add to skillet. Cook and stir till mixture thickens and bubbles. Add celery, green pepper, and tomato; heat through. Serve over Ginger Rice: Toss rice with ginger. Pass additional soy sauce. Makes 2 servings.

QUICK TUNA SKILLET

    ½ 10-ounce package frozen peas and
       onions (about 1 cup)
    ⅓ cup bias-cut celery slices
    1 tablespoon butter or margarine
    1 tablespoon soy sauce
    1 teaspoon cornstarch
    1 cup cooked rice
    1 6½- or 7-ounce can tuna, drained
    ½ 5-ounce can water chestnuts,
       thinly sliced

Combine peas and onions, celery, butter, and ½ cup water; heat to boiling. Cover and simmer 8 to 10 minutes or till vegetables are just tender. Combine soy sauce and cornstarch; add to vegetables; cook and stir till thick and bubbly. Gently stir in remaining ingredients; heat through. Pass extra soy sauce. Serves 2.

BARBECUED BEAN BAKE

Cut one 7-ounce can luncheon meat into 2 or 3 slices. Pour one 16-ounce can baked beans and pork in molasses sauce into small baking dish. Mix 2 tablespoons brown sugar, 2 tablespoons catsup, and 1 tablespoon prepared mustard. Spread some mixture on meat and mix remaining into beans. Arrange meat atop beans in baking dish.

With wooden pick, attach 1 thin slice onion and ½ slice lemon to each meat slice. Bake in moderate oven (375°) for 35 to 40 minutes or till hot. Makes 2 servings.

BRUNCH EGGS RANCHERO

Cut 3 slices bacon into small pieces. In skillet, cook bacon slowly till crisp; drain off excess fat. Add one 8-ounce can tomatoes, cut up, 1 tablespoon chopped green chilies, and ½ clove garlic, minced, to bacon in skillet; heat through. Divide between 2 individual baking dishes. Carefully slip one egg atop tomato mixture in each dish. Sprinkle lightly with salt and pepper. Bake in a slow oven (325°) for 20 to 25 minutes, or till eggs are set. Top each with a crisp bacon curl, if desired. Pass rolled tortillas. Serves 2.

A dish out of the Southwest! Easy Brunch Eggs Ranchero will be a pleasant surprise some morning. You'll welcome the zesty flavor of these eggs. Instead of the usual toast, why not serve rolled buttered tortillas (frozen or canned) with the ramekins of eggs.

PEKING TUNA SALAD

- ¼ cup mayonnaise or salad dressing
- 1 tablespoon minced onion
- 1 teaspoon lemon juice
- 1 teaspoon soy sauce
- ½ teaspoon curry powder
- 1 6½- or 7-ounce can tuna, drained and flaked
- 1 5-ounce can water chestnuts, sliced

Combine mayonnaise, onion, lemon juice, soy, and curry; blend well. Add tuna and water chestnuts; toss mixture gently;* chill. Serve in lettuce cups. Makes 3 or 4 servings.

*Or spread on thin slices of French bread. Broil 2 to 3 inches from heat for 3 to 4 minutes or till heated through.

SOLE-ASPARAGUS BAKE

- 1 10-ounce package frozen asparagus spears, cooked and drained
- ¼ cup tartar sauce*
- 2 frozen sole fillets, thawed
- 2 tablespoons chili sauce

Place asparagus spears in small shallow baking dish. Top with dollops of tartar sauce. Lay thawed fish fillets over top. Spoon chili sauce over fish. Bake in moderate oven (350°) about 30 minutes or till fish flakes easily with a fork. Makes 2 servings.

*Or, use ¼ cup mayonnaise or salad dressing blended with 1 teaspoon pickle relish.

ZIPPY FISH FILLETS

- 1 tablespoon Worcestershire sauce
- 1½ teaspoons lemon juice
- ½ pound fish fillets
  Salt and pepper
- ¼ cup fine dry bread crumbs

Combine Worcestershire and lemon juice. Cut fish in serving-size pieces. Dip pieces in lemon juice mixture, then season with salt and pepper. Dip in bread crumbs. Bake in greased, shallow pan in an extremely hot oven (500°) about 15 minutes. Serve with lemon wedges or tartar sauce. Makes 2 servings.

POACHED SALMON STEAKS WITH CUCUMBER SAUCE

- 2 cups water
- 2 teaspoons salt
- 1 tablespoon lemon juice
- 2 fresh or frozen salmon steaks
  Unpared cucumber
- ½ cup dairy sour cream
- 1 teaspoon minced parsley
- ¼ teaspoon grated onion
- ½ teaspoon lemon juice
- ¼ teaspoon salt
  Dash pepper

In skillet, heat water with 2 teaspoons salt and 1 tablespoon lemon juice to boiling. Add salmon (if using frozen salmon, thaw before cooking). Simmer 12 minutes. Remove steaks with slotted spatula. Chill.

Meanwhile, prepare Cucumber Sauce: Shred enough cucumber to measure ¼ cup (do not drain). Add sour cream, parsley, onion, ½ teaspoon lemon juice, ¼ teaspoon salt, and pepper; blend well. Chill. Arrange salmon on lettuce. Serve with lemon wedges and Cucumber Sauce. Serves 2.

CANTONESE SHRIMP

- 1 tablespoon salad oil
- 1 cup cleaned raw shrimp
- ½ 7-ounce package frozen Chinese pea pods
- 3 tablespoons sliced green onion
- 1 small clove garlic, minced
- ¼ teaspoon monosodium glutamate
- ⅛ teaspoon ground ginger
  • • •
- 1 teaspoon cornstarch
- ½ teaspoon sugar
- ¼ teaspoon salt
- 2 tablespoons cold water
- 1 teaspoon soy sauce

Heat oil in heavy skillet till hot; add shrimp; toss and cook quickly till pink, 3 to 5 minutes. Add pea pods, onion, garlic, monosodium glutamate, and ginger; toss and cook over high heat for 1 minute. Combine remaining ingredients. Pour over shrimp mixture; toss and cook till thick and bubbly, about 1 minute. Pass soy sauce. Makes 2 servings.

Poached Salmon Steaks with Cucumber Sauce will make a hit when the temperature soars! Poach the salmon early in the day so it will be well-chilled by mealtime. The sauce is a cool mixture of shredded cucumber and sour cream. Remember this superbly seasoned sauce for broiled salmon steaks, grilled salmon patties, or on crisp lettuce.

SANDWICHES–GOOD FOR A TWOSOME

BACON BIG BOYS

2 large French rolls
  Prepared mustard
4 slices sharp natural Cheddar
  cheese
4 frankfurters
6 to 8 slices bacon

Split rolls; if tops are rounded, trim slightly. Spread inside of tops with mustard. Arrange 2 cheese slices and 2 frankfurters on bottom half of each. Replace tops. Wrap 3 or 4 bacon slices spiral fashion around each; secure with picks. Place, top down, on rack in shallow pan. Bake at 400° for 5 to 8 minutes. Turn; bake 5 to 8 minutes more. Serves 2.

Bacon Big Boys are hearty, man-sized sandwiches with smokey flavor throughout. Start

"RICH BOY" SANDWICHES

2 large French rolls
3 tablespoons butter or margarine
2 teaspoons prepared mustard
2 slices Bologna
2 slices chopped ham
4 small slices salami
2 slices sharp process American
  cheese, halved diagonally

Split rolls. Blend butter and mustard; spread inside rolls. Arrange 1 slice Bologna, 1 slice chopped ham, 2 slices salami, and 2 cheese triangles on bottom half of each roll. Replace roll tops. Wrap tightly in foil. Heat at 450° for 20 minutes or till hot. Serves 2.

with French rolls from your favorite bakery or use the brown-and-serve type of roll.

PEANUT BUTTER SPECIAL

Butter or margarine, softened
4 slices bread
¼ cup peanut butter
2 tablespoons applesauce
2 slices bacon, crisp-cooked and crumbled (about 1 tablespoon)
½ tart unpared apple, thinly sliced

Butter bread generously. Combine peanut butter, applesauce, and bacon. Spread on 2 slices bread. Top with apple slices, then remaining bread. Cut sandwiches in half; secure with picks if necessary. Makes 2 servings.

BRAUNSCHWEIGER TREATS

4 ounces (½ cup) braunschweiger, softened
¼ cup chopped celery
1 tablespoon chili sauce
2 teaspoons prepared mustard
• • •
4 slices rye bread, toasted
2 slices sharp process American cheese, halved diagonally

Combine braunschweiger, celery, chili sauce, and mustard; spread on toast. Broil 3 to 4 minutes. Top with cheese triangles. Return to broiler to melt cheese. Makes 2 servings.

CURRIED CHICKEN-WICHES

2 large slices cooked chicken
2 slices buttered toast
• • •
3 tablespoons mayonnaise or salad dressing
¼ cup finely chopped unpared apple
2 tablespoons finely chopped celery
¼ teaspoon curry powder
Dash *each* salt and pepper

Arrange chicken on toast. Combine remaining ingredients; spread evenly over chicken to edges of toast. Place on baking pan. Heat at 400° for 10 minutes. Serves 2.

HAM AND EGG ROLLS

½ cup chopped cooked ham
¼ cup diced sharp process American cheese
1 tablespoon sliced green onion
1 hard-cooked egg, chopped
2 tablespoons sliced pimiento-stuffed green olives
2 tablespoons mayonnaise or salad dressing
2 tablespoons chili sauce
4 hamburger buns, split and buttered

Combine all ingredients except buns. Spread mixture in buns. Wrap in foil. Heat at 400° for 15 to 20 minutes. Makes 4 sandwiches.

BROILED TURKEY BUNS

1 cup chopped cooked turkey
¼ cup chopped celery
3 tablespoons mayonnaise or salad dressing
2 teaspoons finely chopped onion
1 teaspoon lemon juice
• • •
2 hamburger buns, split, toasted, and buttered
2 slices sharp process American cheese, halved diagonally

Combine first 5 ingredients; add salt and pepper to taste. Spread on bun halves, covering to edges. Broil 3 to 4 inches from heat 2 to 3 minutes. Top with cheese; broil till melted. Makes 4 open-face sandwiches.

DUTCH LUNCH

⅔ cup chopped cabbage
2 tablespoons mayonnaise
½ teaspoon prepared mustard
2 tablespoons chopped pimiento-stuffed green olives
4 slices rye bread, buttered
4 thin slices boiled ham

Combine cabbage, mayonnaise, mustard, and olives. Top 2 *slices* bread with ham, then cabbage mixture. Top with remaining bread.

ROAST BEEF CHAMPIONS

        4   slices dark rye bread
            Butter or margarine, softened
      ¼   cup dairy sour cream
        1   teaspoon *dry* onion soup mix
        1   teaspoon prepared horseradish,
                well drained
            Dash freshly ground pepper
            Thinly sliced cold roast beef
            Leaf lettuce

Spread bread slices with butter. Combine sour cream, onion soup mix, horseradish, and pepper. Spread on bread. Top 2 slices with roast beef, then lettuce; cover with remaining 2 slices bread. Makes 2 sandwiches.

CHEESE FRANK ROLL-UPS

        1   tube refrigerated biscuits
                (6 biscuits)
            Prepared mustard
            Pickle relish
        2   slices sharp process American
                cheese, halved
        4   frankfurters

Pat four of the biscuits to 4-inch circles. Spread with mustard and pickle relish. Top with cheese slice, then frankfurter. Roll biscuits around franks; place, seam side down, on baking sheet. Bake at 375° for 12 minutes. Bake extra biscuits plain. Serves 2.

CHEESE BUNS DELUXE

        2   ounces sharp process
            American cheese, shredded (½ cup)
        2   tablespoons mayonnaise or salad
                dressing
        2   tablespoons chopped ripe olives
        1   tablespoon chopped green onion
      ⅛   teaspoon curry powder
        2   hamburger buns, split and
                toasted

Combine cheese, mayonnaise or salad dressing, olives, onion, and curry powder; spread on toasted bun halves. Broil 4 inches from heat for about 2 minutes or till cheese melts. Makes 4 open-face sandwiches.

PEKING HAMBURGERS

      ½   pound ground beef
        1   8½-ounce can pineapple slices
        3   tablespoons brown sugar
        1   teaspoon cornstarch
    1½   tablespoons red wine vinegar
    1½   teaspoons soy sauce
    1½   teaspoons Worcestershire sauce
            • • •
        2   green pepper rings
        2   hamburger buns, split and
                toasted

Shape ground beef into 2 patties; sprinkle with salt and pepper. Broil about 4 inches from heat for 10 minutes, turning once.

Meanwhile, drain pineapple, reserving 2 tablespoons syrup. Combine brown sugar and cornstarch in small saucepan; blend in pineapple syrup, wine vinegar, soy sauce, and Worcestershire sauce. Cook and stir till mixture comes to boiling. Add 2 pineapple slices; top each with green pepper ring. Cover and heat through. Place broiled beef patties on buns; top with pineapple and green pepper. Spoon a little sauce over. Trim plate with remaining pineapple slices. Makes 2 sandwiches.

SHRIMP CURRY LUNCHEON

        1   avocado, peeled and sliced
        1   tablespoon lime juice
            • • •
    1½   teaspoons butter or margarine
      ½   teaspoon curry powder
      ½   teaspoon salt
        1   small tomato, peeled and chopped
                (½ cup)
        2   tablespoons chopped onion
      ¾   cup cleaned cooked shrimp
      ½   cup dairy sour cream
        2   English muffins, split and
                toasted

Brush avocado slices with lime juice; heat in slow oven (300°) 5 to 10 minutes.

Melt butter in small saucepan; add curry, salt, tomato, and onion. Cook till onion is tender, about 5 minutes. Add shrimp; heat through. Stir in sour cream; heat through but *do not boil.* Top muffin halves with warm avocado; spoon shrimp curry over. Serves 2.

AVOCADO OPEN-FACERS

  3 tablespoons mayonnaise or salad
     dressing
  1 tablespoon lemon juice
  4 slices whole wheat bread,
     toasted
  1 avocado, peeled and sliced
     Leaf lettuce
  1 tomato, thinly sliced
  8 slices bacon, crisp-cooked and
     drained
     Thousand Island salad dressing

Combine mayonnaise and *half* the lemon juice; spread on one side of each slice toast. Brush avocado with remaining lemon juice. Place leaf lettuce, tomato slices, and avocado slices on toast. Sprinkle with salt and pepper. Crisscross 2 bacon slices atop each. Spoon on Thousand Island dressing. Garnish plate with relishes. Makes 4 open-face sandwiches.

FRANK BEANWICHES

Saucy, hot sandwiches for a chilly-day lunch—

  ½ 11-ounce can Boston brown bread,
     cut in 4 slices
     Butter or margarine, softened
  1 9-ounce can pork and beans in
     tomato sauce
  1 tablespoon catsup
  1 teaspoon prepared mustard
  ¼ teaspoon instant minced onion
  2 frankfurters, split lengthwise
  ¼ cup shredded sharp natural Cheddar
     cheese

Spread bread with butter; place 2 slices on each luncheon plate. In small skillet, combine pork and beans, catsup, mustard, and instant minced onion; mix. Add franks; cover and cook over low heat for 10 minutes. Spoon mixture over brown bread slices; top with shredded cheese. Makes 2 servings.

Elegant summer luncheon

Avocado Open-facers are a knife-and-fork version of the popular all-time favorite—bacon-lettuce-tomato sandwich.

THESE SWEETS ARE A SNAP

PINK VELVET SHERBET

1   10-ounce package frozen strawberries, partially thawed
1   cup crushed ice
1   6-ounce can (⅔ cup) evaporated milk
½   cup sugar
1   tablespoon lemon juice

Break fruit apart into chunks. Place all ingredients in blender container. Blend at high speed 2 minutes or till thick. Freeze, covered, in refrigerator tray. Makes 3 servings.

QUICK APPLE PIELETS

Cheese fans might like to add a little finely shredded Cheddar to the pastry—

1   stick pie crust mix
2   medium tart apples, pared, cored, and sliced (2 cups)
⅓   cup sugar
⅓   cup water
1   teaspoon lemon juice
¼   teaspoon ground cinnamon
1   tablespoon cornstarch
1   tablespoon cold water

Prepare pie crust mix according to package directions. Roll to 12x6-inch rectangle; cut into 3-inch squares with pastry wheel or knife. Prick with fork. Bake on baking sheet at 450° for 8 to 10 minutes or till lightly browned.

Combine apples, sugar, water, lemon juice, and cinnamon in small saucepan. Cook over medium heat, stirring once or twice, for 5 minutes or till tender. Combine cornstarch and cold water; stir into apple mixture. Cook and stir till thickened and bubbly.

Remove from heat; cool. For each serving, spoon some filling between two pastry squares; top each with more filling. Serve with ice cream or whipped cream. Makes 2 servings.

Note: Use extra pastry squares as base for creamed chicken or turkey.

JAVA EGGNOG

1   egg
1   teaspoon instant coffee powder
¼   teaspoon vanilla
    Dash salt
3   tablespoons sugar
1   cup milk
½   cup whipping cream, whipped

Beat egg till thick; add coffee powder, vanilla, and salt. Gradually beat in sugar. Stir in milk, then stir in whipped cream. Pour into cups; sprinkle with a dash of ground nutmeg, if desired. Makes 2⅔ cups.

PEANUT RAISIN LOGS

½   cup peanut butter
½   cup light corn syrup
½   cup nonfat dry milk powder
½   cup confectioners' sugar
½   cup raisins

Mix peanut butter, corn syrup, dry milk, and sugar. Add raisins; mix well. Chill candy mixture. Divide into 24 pieces; form each into small log. Wrap individually in clear plastic wrap. Keep refrigerated.

THREE-FRUIT SHERBET

Made easily with a blender—

1   medium fully ripe banana
½   6-ounce can (⅓ cup) frozen orange juice concentrate, partially thawed
1   13¼-ounce can pineapple tidbits, undrained
½   cup whipping cream

Combine ingredients in blender container. Switch blender on and off till well blended. Pile into freezer tray; cover and freeze till firm. Serve in sherbet glasses. Serves 3 or 4.

RUBY FRUIT COMPOTE

1 20-ounce can frozen pitted
   tart red cherries, thawed
⅓ cup sugar
1 tablespoon cornstarch
   Dash salt
1 teaspoon lemon juice
1 cup whole fresh strawberries, rinsed
   and hulled
   Dairy sour cream

Drain cherries, reserving syrup. Add enough water to syrup to measure 1¼ cups. Blend sugar, cornstarch, and salt in saucepan; add reserved syrup. Cook and stir till thick and bubbly. Add lemon juice. Stir in cherries and strawberries. Chill thoroughly.

Spoon into sherbet glasses. Top with dollop of dairy sour cream. Refrigerate extra fruit mixture; use as cake or ice cream topper.

CARAMEL STACK-UPS

Fold 1 tablespoon caramel sundae topping into ½ cup whipping cream, whipped. Frost 8 chocolate wafers with some whipped cream mixture. Stack frosted cookies 4 high; frost sides. Chill several hours. Drizzle with extra sundae topping before serving. Serves 2.

PEANUT COCO-ROONS

1⅓ cups flaked coconut
½ cup sweetened *condensed* milk
   Dash salt
1 teaspoon vanilla
1 square (1 ounce) unsweetened
   chocolate, melted
¾ cup coarsely chopped peanuts

Combine all ingredients; mix well. Drop from teaspoon onto greased baking sheet, 1 inch apart. Bake at 350° for 8 to 10 minutes. Remove from baking sheet at once. Makes 24.

Midsummer fruit refresher

Ruby Fruit Compote will steal the scene as a brunch starter or anytime-dessert. It's easy, beautiful, and so delicious!

MEALS TO DOUBLE-UP AND DIVIDE

Cook once for twice—or more. If you have ample freezer space, leftovers will be a blessing, not a problem. With a little advance planning, you can have a variety of delicious foods on standby with very little extra effort.

You'll notice an emphasis on meat dishes in this chapter. We've included a menu featuring a large grilled ham slice supplemented by several recipes calling for cooked ham. And there's a similar section on turkey. Or dress up meatballs four different ways. Wise planning, buying, and cooking in the meat area will save you the most in dollars and hours.

Bread, rolls, and desserts also let you make good use of your freezer space. Here you'll find a two-way coffee cake recipe, cookies that freeze well, sherbets, ice cream toppers, and drinks. Start with the recipes and suggestions in this chapter—you'll soon be devising your own time- and work-saving schemes.

Meatballs in Barbecue Sauce, Meatball Stroganoff, Meatballs in Sauerbraten Sauce, and Spaghetti 'n Meatballs—make all 4 meals from Oven Meatballs.

MENU

Late Night Snack

Oven Meatballs in Barbecue Sauce
Miniature Hamburger Buns
Potato Chips
Crisp Relishes
Fresh Fruit and Cheese
Coffee

MENU

Special Meal in Minutes

Meatball Stroganoff
Noodles
Deviled Green Beans
Lettuce Wedges   *French Dressing*
Lemon Sherbet
Coffee

OVEN MEATBALLS

Prepare four delicious meals at one time! Keep meatballs on standby in freezer—

 2 pounds ground beef
 1½ cups soft bread crumbs (3 slices bread)
 ½ cup milk
 ¼ cup finely chopped onion
 2 eggs
 1½ teaspoons salt

Combine all ingredients; mix lightly but thoroughly. Shape into 4 dozen *small* balls, about 1 inch in diameter. Place in 15½x10½x 1-inch baking pan. Brown in moderate oven (375°) 25 to 30 minutes. Divide meatballs into 4 portions. Wrap 3 portions separately in foil and freeze. Serve remaining meatballs in Barbecue Sauce (below).

BARBECUE SAUCE

 ½ cup catsup
 2 tablespoons butter or margarine
 2 tablespoons light molasses
 1 tablespoon vinegar
 2 tablespoons water

Combine all ingredients in saucepan. Simmer uncovered for 15 minutes. *Add ¼ recipe (12) Oven Meatballs (above); heat through. Serve in chafing dish, if desired. Makes 2 servings.

*Or cool sauce; add ¼ of meatballs; freeze to serve another time.

MEATBALL STROGANOFF

 ¼ cup chopped onion
 2 tablespoons butter or margarine
 1 tablespoon all-purpose flour
 ¾ cup *condensed* beef broth
 1 tablespoon sherry
 1 tablespoon catsup
 ¼ recipe (12) Oven Meatballs
 ¼ cup dairy sour cream
 Hot cooked noodles

In small saucepan, cook onion in butter till tender but not brown. Stir in flour. Add broth, wine, and catsup. Cook and stir till mixture bubbles. Add frozen or not frozen meatballs; cover; cook over low heat 6 to 8 minutes (not frozen), or 10 to 12 minutes (frozen); stir occasionally. Stir in sour cream. Heat, but *do not boil.* Serve over noodles. Makes 2 servings.

DEVILED GREEN BEANS

 1 8-ounce can cut green beans
 • • •
 1½ teaspoons butter or margarine
 1 teaspoon prepared mustard
 ½ teaspoon Worcestershire sauce
 Dash salt
 Dash pepper

In a saucepan heat green beans; drain thoroughly. In small saucepan melt butter or margarine. Stir in mustard, Worcestershire sauce, salt, and pepper. Pour over hot beans; stir gently. Makes 2 servings.

```
⤙ MENU ⤚

"Deutsch" Dinner

Meatballs in Sauerbraten Sauce
Buttered Rice              Broccoli Spears
        Raspberry Ring
Brown 'n Serve Rolls            Butter
     German Chocolate Cake
              Coffee
```

```
⤙ MENU ⤚

Speedy Supper

     Spaghetti 'n Meatballs
Green Salad            Italian Dressing
          Bread Sticks
Angel Cake          Apricot-almond Sauce
          Red Wine
          Coffee
```

SAUERBRATEN SAUCE

    ¾ cup water
    1 beef bouillon cube
    3 tablespoons brown sugar
    2 tablespoons raisins
    2 tablespoons lemon juice
    ¼ cup coarse gingersnap crumbs
    ¼ recipe (12) Oven Meatballs
      Hot cooked rice

Bring water and bouillon cube to boiling. Add remaining ingredients except meatballs and rice. Cook and stir to dissolve gingersnaps. Add frozen or not frozen meatballs. Cook, covered, over low heat for about 15 minutes, stirring occasionally. Serve over fluffy hot cooked rice. Makes 2 servings.

RASPBERRY RING

    1 3-ounce package lemon-flavored
      gelatin
    1 cup boiling water
    1 10-ounce package frozen rasp-
      berries, thawed and sieved
    ¼ cup port wine
    ¾ cup seedless green grapes,
      halved

Dissolve gelatin in boiling water; stir in sieved raspberries (pulp and juice) and wine. Chill till partially set; fold in grapes. Pour into 3-cup mold; chill till set. Serve on greens. Garnish each serving with tiny bunch of grapes. Makes 4 servings.

SPAGHETTI 'N MEATBALLS

    2 tablespoons chopped onion
    2 tablespoons chopped green pepper
    1 tablespoon salad oil
              • • •
    1 8-ounce can (1 cup) tomatoes,
      cut up
    ½ cup tomato sauce
    1 3-ounce can chopped mushrooms,
      drained (½ cup)
    1 teaspoon brown sugar
    ¼ teaspoon dried oregano, crushed
    ¼ teaspoon dried basil, crushed
    ¼ teaspoon garlic salt
              • • •
    ¼ recipe (12) Oven Meatballs
      Hot cooked spaghetti
      Grated Parmesan cheese

In medium saucepan, cook onion and green pepper in oil till tender but not brown. Add next 7 ingredients; mix well. Add frozen or not frozen meatballs. Simmer, uncovered, 20 to 30 minutes, stirring occasionally. Serve over hot cooked spaghetti. Pass grated Parmesan cheese. Makes 2 servings.

APRICOT-ALMOND SAUCE

Lightly brown 1 tablespoon chopped almonds in 1 tablespoon butter or margarine over low heat. Add ⅓ cup apricot preserves and 1 tablespoon lemon juice; heat till preserves are melted. Serve over cake and/or ice cream. Makes ½ cup sauce.

⟜ *MENU* ⟝

Luncheon Tray

Turkey Open-facers
Fresh Fruit Salad
Assorted Relishes
Chocolate Velvet Sundaes
Coffee

TURKEY OPEN-FACERS

¼ cup clear French salad
   dressing with herbs and spices
1 tablespoon chopped onion
⅛ teaspoon pepper
½ 12-ounce package frozen asparagus spears, cooked and drained *or*
   6 fresh asparagus spears, cooked
   and drained
1 tablespoon butter, softened
2 teaspoons mayonnaise
2 slices white bread, toasted
4 slices cooked turkey
2 slices process Swiss cheese

Management memo:

- Cook a boneless turkey roll to slice for the turkey sandwiches. Then freeze extra meat for the turkey recipes on opposite page.
- Sprinkle peaches, apples, bananas, and pears with ascorbic acid color keeper, or drizzle with lemon juice and water mixture to keep colors bright in fresh fruit salads.

Combine French dressing, onion, and pepper. Pour over asparagus in saucepan; bring to boiling. Blend butter and mayonnaise; spread on toast. Top with turkey, then asparagus. Halve cheese slices diagonally; place atop asparagus. Broil till cheese melts. Serves 2.

Turkey Open-facers are a show-off use for those first tender stalks of fresh asparagus —and so delicious, you'll keep making them all summer long! Great for calorie-counters because there's only half as much bread as in the ordinary two-slice sandwich.

CHOCOLATE VELVET SAUCE

    1 6-ounce package (1 cup) semi-
      sweet chocolate pieces
    ⅔ cup light corn syrup
    1 6-ounce can (⅔ cup) evaporated
      milk

In saucepan, combine chocolate pieces and corn syrup; cook and stir over low heat till chocolate melts. Remove from heat; cool. Stir in evaporated milk. Serve warm or cold over vanilla ice cream. Store extra sauce covered in refrigerator. Makes 1⅔ cups.

TURKEY-CHEESE PUFFS

    ½ 10-ounce package frozen chopped
      broccoli
    1 cup diced cooked turkey
    1 10¾-ounce can chicken gravy
    1 egg
    2 tablespoons grated Parmesan
      cheese
    2 tablespoons toasted slivered
      almonds

Cook and drain broccoli; place in 2 individual casseroles. Cover with turkey; top with gravy. Bake uncovered at 375° for 15 minutes or till hot. Beat egg and dash salt till thick; fold in cheese. Spoon over turkey; top with almonds. Bake at 375° for 10 minutes. Serves 2.

TURKEY HASH

    ¼ cup finely chopped onion
    1 tablespoon butter or margarine
    1 3-ounce can chopped mushrooms,
      drained
    1 cup diced cooked turkey
    1 cup diced cooked potato
    ¾ teaspoon seasoned salt
      Dash pepper
    ⅓ cup milk

In small saucepan, cook onion in butter till tender but not brown. Remove from heat and stir in mushrooms, turkey, potato, seasoned salt, and pepper. Add the milk, stirring gently. Heat mixture; place in serving dish. Garnish with snipped parsley. Makes 2 servings.

TURKEY SALAD BAKE

    1½ cups cubed cooked turkey
    ½ cup sliced celery
    ¼ cup toasted slivered almonds
    ¼ teaspoon salt
    ¼ teaspoon monosodium glutamate
    ¼ teaspoon grated onion
    2 teaspoons lemon juice
    ½ cup mayonnaise or salad dressing
       • • •
    2 tablespoons grated Parmesan
      cheese
    ½ cup soft bread crumbs
    1 tablespoon butter, melted

Combine all ingredients except cheese, crumbs, and butter. Pile lightly into 2 shallow individual casseroles. Combine cheese, crumbs, and melted butter; sprinkle over turkey mixture. Bake in hot oven (425°) for 20 to 25 minutes or till heated through. Serves 2.

BEEF MUSHROOM LOAF

    1 2-ounce can chopped
      mushrooms
      Milk
    1 slightly beaten egg
    1 teaspoon Worcestershire sauce
    ¾ teaspoon salt
    ½ teaspoon dry mustard
      Dash pepper
    1 cup soft bread crumbs
    1 pound lean ground beef
    2 tablespoons catsup
    1 tablespoon light corn syrup

Drain mushrooms, reserving liquid; add enough milk to make ½ cup. In bowl, combine liquid and all ingredients *except* catsup and corn syrup. Mix well; divide mixture in half. Pat each portion into 5½x3x2¼-inch loaf pan or shape in loaf in baking pan.

Bake one loaf in moderate oven (350°) for 40 minutes. Combine catsup and corn syrup; spoon *half* of mixture over loaf. Bake 10 minutes more. Makes 2 servings.

Freeze other loaf; refrigerate extra glaze. To serve frozen loaf, bake at 350° for 1 hour and 10 minutes. Spoon other half of catsup-corn syrup mixture over top; bake 10 minutes more. Makes 2 servings.

Patio Dinner

Gingered Ham Slice
Hot Deviled Potatoes   *Buttered Peas*
Fresh Fruit   *French Dressing*
Poppy Seed Rolls
Lime Sherbet   *Coconut Macaroons*
Iced Tea or *Coffee*

GINGERED HAM SLICE

  1 fully cooked center cut ham
     slice, 1 inch thick
½ cup ginger ale
½ cup orange juice
¼ cup brown sugar
  1 tablespoon salad oil
1½ teaspoons wine vinegar
  1 teaspoon dry mustard
¼ teaspoon ground ginger
⅛ teaspoon ground cloves

Slash fat edge of ham. Combine remaining ingredients; pour over ham in shallow dish. Refrigerate overnight or let stand at room temperature 2 hours, spooning marinade over ham several times. Heat in a moderate oven (350°) about 30 minutes, brushing frequently with marinade. Or, broil over low coals about 15 minutes on each side, brushing often. To serve, spoon remaining marinade over ham. Makes 5 or 6 servings.

HOT DEVILED POTATOES

    Packaged instant mashed potatoes
¼ cup dairy sour cream
½ teaspoon prepared mustard
¼ teaspoon sugar
  1 tablespoon snipped green onion

Prepare 2 servings potatoes according to package directions. Stir in remaining ingredients. Spoon into 2 foil baking shells. Sprinkle with paprika. Bake at 350° about 20 minutes, or till heated through. Serves 2.

BUYING GUIDE FOR HAM

Purchase a small half fully-cooked ham. Have meatman cut off center slice 1-inch thick for Gingered Ham Slice. Leftover ham slice makes great sandwiches. Cube remaining half ham for main dishes, such as those below.

Uses for leftover ham:

HAM AND RICE BAKE

½ 10½-ounce can condensed cream of
    mushroom soup (about ⅔ cup)
⅔ cup water
  1 cup cubed cooked ham
⅔ cup uncooked packaged precooked
    rice
  1 8-ounce can green beans, drained
  1 tablespoon chopped onion
  3 tablespoons fine dry bread crumbs
  1 teaspoon butter, melted

Combine all ingredients except crumbs and butter in a saucepan. Heat till boiling. Pour into a 1-quart casserole. Toss crumbs with butter; sprinkle over casserole. Bake at 400° about 20 minutes. Makes 2 servings.

HAM BARBECUE

  1 cup cubed cooked ham
  1 teaspoon salad oil
  1 8¾-ounce can pineapple tidbits
¼ cup bottled barbecue sauce
1½ teaspoons cornstarch
½ medium green pepper, cut in strips
    Hot cooked rice

Brown meat lightly in hot oil in skillet. Drain pineapple, reserving syrup. Stir syrup and barbecue sauce into browned meat. Cover; simmer 10 minutes. Blend cornstarch with ⅓ cup cold water; stir into meat. Cook and stir till thickened and bubbly. Add the pineapple and the green pepper. Heat through. Serve over rice. Makes 2 servings.

Two-way ginger-marinated ham

Gingered Ham Slice goes over the coals for →
a special backyard barbecue or into the
oven for a delicious midwinter meal.

⟨ *MENU* ⟩

Midmorning Breakfast

Fruit Wake-up
Cereal with Eggnog Topper
Caramel Pecan Rolls
or
Cinnamon Crescent
Coffee

FRUIT WAKE-UP

Pretend you're having breakfast in the tropics—

1 small banana, sliced (1 cup)
1 8-ounce can pineapple tidbits, drained
⅓ cup orange juice
2 tablespoons toasted coconut (optional)

Combine banana, pineapple, and orange juice; chill. (Be sure banana is covered entirely with juice.) Spoon into dishes; top each serving with coconut, if desired. Makes 2 servings.

EGGNOG CEREAL TOPPER

Egg, milk, and cereal all in one bowl!—

1 egg
Dash salt
1 cup milk
2 tablespoons maple-blended *or* maple-flavored syrup
Ready-to-eat cereal

Combine egg, salt, milk, and maple syrup; blend thoroughly. Serve over cereal.

The fragrance of homemade rolls

← Caramel Pecan Rolls are everyone's favorite! They're wonderful for breakfast or paired with a big mug of coffee for that midmorning break. Freeze any leftover rolls.

TWO-WAY COFFEE CAKE

1 package active dry yeast
⅓ cup milk, scalded
2 tablespoons granulated sugar
2 tablespoons shortening
½ teaspoon salt
1¾ cups sifted all-purpose flour
1 egg
• • •
Roll Topper
2 tablespoons butter, melted
¼ cup granulated sugar
½ teaspoon ground cinnamon
Cinnamon Crescent topper

Soften yeast in ¼ cup warm water (110°). Combine milk, 2 tablespoons sugar, shortening, and salt; cool to lukewarm. Add *1 cup* of the flour; beat well. Beat in softened yeast and egg. Gradually add remaining flour to form soft dough, beating well. Cover and let rise in warm place till double, 1½ to 2 hours. Chill dough for easier handling.

For *Roll Topper,* in small saucepan, combine ⅓ cup brown sugar, 2 tablespoons butter, and 1 tablespoon corn syrup. Cook and stir just till butter melts and mixture is blended. Distribute evenly in bottom of 6 greased muffin cups; top with 3 tablespoons pecan halves.

Divide dough in half. On lightly floured surface, roll each piece to 9x6-inch rectangle. Brush each rectangle with *half* the melted butter. Combine ¼ cup sugar and cinnamon; sprinkle *half* over each rectangle of dough.

For **Caramel Pecan Rolls:** Roll up *one* piece dough, jelly-roll style, beginning with long side; seal edges. Cut into six slices. Place rolls, cut side down, in prepared muffin pan. Cover; let rise in warm place till double, 30 to 45 minutes. Bake in a moderate oven (375°) for 15 to 18 minutes. Cool about 30 seconds; invert on rack; remove pan. Makes 6 rolls.

For **Cinnamon Crescent:** Sprinkle *second* rectangle of dough with 1 teaspoon water; spread with spatula. Sprinkle with ¼ cup raisins and 2 tablespoons chopped pecans. Roll up, jelly-roll style, beginning with long side; seal edge. Place, sealed side down, on greased baking sheet. Curve to form crescent; pinch each end to seal. Cover; let rise in warm place till double, 30 to 45 minutes. Bake at 375° for 12 to 15 minutes. Cool; frost crescent with confectioners' icing.

DESSERT...ON CALL

COCONUT ICE CREAM

In saucepan, combine one 14½-ounce can evaporated milk and ½ cup sugar; cook and stir till sugar dissolves; cool. Stir in 2 teaspoons vanilla. Freeze, covered, in 11x7x1½-inch pan. Place in chilled bowl; break up. Beat smooth. Fold in 1 cup whipping cream, whipped, and ⅔ cup flaked coconut, toasted. Freeze.

PEANUT BUTTER BROWNIES

- ¼ cup butter or margarine
- 2 squares (2 ounces) unsweetened chocolate
- 1 cup sugar
- ¼ cup chunk-style peanut butter
- ½ teaspoon vanilla
- 2 eggs
- ½ cup sifted all-purpose flour

Melt butter and chocolate over low heat; cool. Blend in sugar, peanut butter, ¼ teaspoon salt, and vanilla. Beat in eggs, one at a time. Stir in flour. Spread in greased 8x8x2-inch pan. Bake at 350° about 25 minutes.

Wrap extra brownies in moisture-vapor-proof material; seal. Label with contents, date. Freeze. Thaw in wrap at room temperature.

BUTTER BALLS

Cream together 1 cup butter or margarine, ½ cup brown sugar, and 1 teaspoon vanilla till light and fluffy. Gradually add 2¼ cups sifted all-purpose flour, mixing till smooth. Form into 1-inch balls; roll in granulated sugar. Bake on greased cookie sheet at 325° for 20 minutes. Cool. Freeze extra cookies. Makes 48.

LEMON-RAISIN DROPS

- ½ cup butter or margarine
- ¾ cup sugar
- 1 egg
- 2 tablespoons milk
- ½ teaspoon lemon extract
- 1¾ cups sifted all-purpose flour
- ¾ teaspoon cream of tartar
- ¾ teaspoon soda
- ¼ teaspoon salt
- ½ cup raisins

Cream butter and sugar; beat in egg, milk, and extract; mix well. Sift together dry ingredients; stir into creamed mixture. Stir in raisins. Drop from teaspoon onto cookie sheet. Bake at 400° for 10 to 12 minutes. Cool. Freeze extra cookies. Makes 30 to 36.

To keep ice cream crystal free, exclude all the air. Either wrap and seal carton in plastic bag or transfer to plastic box.

Keep dollops of whipped cream on standby in the freezer. Freeze mounds on waxed paper or foil, then transfer to plastic bag.

NECTARINE SHERBET

   1 envelope (1 tablespoon) un-
      flavored gelatin
   1 cup sugar
1¼ cups milk
1½ pounds fresh nectarines (about 6)
   2 tablespoons lemon juice
   1 egg white

Combine gelatin, sugar, and ⅛ teaspoon salt
in saucepan. Stir in milk. Stir over low heat
till gelatin dissolves; cool. Peel, slice, and
puree or *very finely* chop nectarines; stir in
lemon juice. Stir nectarine mixture into gelatin mixture; mix thoroughly. Add a few
drops red food coloring, if desired. Pour into
9x9x2-inch pan or 2 refrigerator trays; cover
and freeze till almost firm.

    Turn into chilled bowl; add unbeaten egg
white. Beat with electric or rotary beater till
smooth and fluffy. Return to pan; freeze 4
hours or till firm. Remove from freezer 10 minutes before serving. Trim with mint.

CINNAMON DIAMONDS

   1 cup butter or margarine
   1 cup brown sugar
   1 egg yolk
  ½ teaspoon vanilla
   2 cups sifted all-purpose flour
   1 teaspoon ground cinnamon
   1 slightly beaten egg white
  ¾ cup chopped walnuts

Cream butter and brown sugar together till
light. Beat in egg yolk and vanilla. Sift together flour and cinnamon; stir into creamed mixture. Pat dough into ungreased 15½x10½x1-
inch baking pan. Brush with egg white; sprinkle with nuts. Press nuts lightly into surface.
Bake in moderate oven (350°) for 18 to 20
minutes. Cut into diamonds; cool; remove
from pan. Freeze extra cookies in moisture-
vaporproof wrap. Makes about 4 dozen.

Nice to have in the freezer

Capture the delicate flavor of ripe fruit in
this refreshing Nectarine Sherbet—perfect
ending for a summer meal with cookies.

MINT FUDGE TOPPING

½ 6-ounce package (½ cup) semi-
sweet mint-flavored chocolate
pieces
⅓ cup milk
½ cup marshmallow creme

Combine mint-flavored chocolate pieces and milk in small saucepan. Heat slowly, stirring till blended. Beat in marshmallow creme till blended. Serve warm or cold over vanilla ice cream. Top with toasted sliced almonds. Makes about 1 cup sauce.

CHERRY-CHOCOLATE BALLS

1 8-ounce can pitted dark sweet
cherries
2 tablespoons brandy or cognac
1 pint chocolate ice cream
¼ cup finely chopped nuts

Drain cherries, reserving syrup. Cook syrup in 1-quart saucepan till reduced to ¼ cup. Add brandy and cherries. Let stand 6 to 8 hours or overnight. Drain cherries. Fill small ice cream scoop or ¼-cup measure with chocolate ice cream; poke 2 or 3 cherries into center. Cover with ice cream to make a ball; freeze. Let balls soften slightly before serving; roll in chopped nuts. Makes 2 or 3 servings.

COFFEE SHERBET

1¼ cups sugar
1 tablespoon unflavored gelatin
4 teaspoons instant coffee powder
Dash salt
2 cups milk
1 cup whipping cream
1 teaspoon vanilla

Combine sugar, gelatin, coffee powder, and salt in saucepan. Stir in 1½ cups cold water; stir over low heat till gelatin dissolves. Remove from heat. Add milk, cream, and vanilla; mix well. Pour mixture into 6-cup refrigerator tray. Cover and freeze till firm.

Remove to chilled mixer bowl; break into chunks. Beat till smooth but still mushy; return to tray; cover and freeze till firm.

PINEAPPLE-LEMON FIZZ

¾ cup pineapple juice, chilled
1 cup vanilla ice cream
½ cup lemon sherbet
½ teaspoon bitters
1 7-ounce bottle lemon-lime
carbonated beverage, chilled

In mixer bowl or blender container, combine pineapple juice, ice cream, sherbet, and bitters. Beat or blend till smooth. Pour into 2 tall glasses; carefully pour in carbonated beverage; stir gently. Serves 2.

CREAM PUFFS

¼ cup butter or margarine
½ cup sifted all-purpose flour
Dash salt
2 eggs

Melt butter in ½ cup boiling water. Add flour and salt all at once; stir vigorously. Cook and stir till mixture forms a ball that doesn't separate. Remove from heat; cool slightly. Add eggs, one at a time, beating after each till smooth. Drop by heaping tablespoons 3 inches apart on greased cookie sheet.

Bake at 450° for 15 minutes, then at 325° for 25 minutes. Remove from oven; split; remove excess moist membrane. Turn oven off; put cream puffs back in to dry, about 20 minutes. Cool on rack. Wrap extra cream puffs tightly in moisture-vaporproof material; label with contents and date; freeze. To serve, fill with pudding, whipped cream, or ice cream and top with favorite sauce. Makes 4 or 5.

JUBILEE SAUCE

Combine one 16-ounce jar dark cherry preserves with ¼ cup port wine and ¼ teaspoon almond extract; chill. Serve over ice cream or filled cream puffs. Makes 1⅔ cups.

Have your own ice cream social

Serve Pineapple-lemon Fizz, Mint Fudge →
Topping, or "dressed up" cones. They'll turn ice cream eating into an occasion.

EASY ON THE BUDGET MAIN DISHES

Low-cost meals can be delicious. You don't have to limit your menus to fit them into your budget. By buying the lower-cost meat cuts, you can serve beef, lamb, chicken, or fish prepared in dishes that will rival filet or lobster. In fact, you may find yourself spending less at the grocery store while eating a greater variety of foods.

Especially valuable from both a cost and nutrition standpoint are egg and cheese dishes. We've included a primer on basic egg cookery as well as some brand-new egg and cheese combinations.

No one will complain if you choose to keep costs in line by serving that "sweetheart of the meat case"—ground beef. Here you'll find a whole array of extra-special burger suggestions. Add one or several of these burgers to your list of foods to fix again and again for low-cost meals.

Oven Beef Stew smells and tastes like a chef's masterpiece—and couldn't be easier. The savory gravy is made with tomato soup and red wine.

ECONOMICAL ENTREES

OVEN BEEF STEW

    1 tablespoon all-purpose flour
    ¾ teaspoon salt
      Dash pepper
    ¾ pound beef chuck, cut in
      1-inch cubes
    1 tablespoon shortening
    1 10½-ounce can condensed
      tomato soup
    1 soup can water (1¼ cups)
    ¾ cup chopped onion
    ¼ teaspoon dried basil, crushed
    2 medium potatoes, pared and cubed
    2 medium carrots, cut in 1-inch
      pieces
    ¼ cup dry red wine or water

Combine flour, salt, and pepper; coat meat cubes in seasoned flour. Brown in hot shortening in small Dutch oven; add soup, water, onion, and basil. Cover and bake in moderate oven (375°) about 1 hour. Add potatoes, carrots, and wine. Cover and bake 1 hour longer or till tender. Makes 2 or 3 servings.

BRAISED LAMB SHANKS

    2 tablespoons all-purpose flour
    ¼ teaspoon salt
    2 medium lamb shanks
    1 tablespoon salad oil
    ½ cup chopped onion
    1 small clove garlic, minced
    ¾ cup water
    1 tablespoon snipped parsley
    ¼ teaspoon salt
    ¼ teaspoon curry powder
      Dash cayenne

Combine flour, ¼ teaspoon salt, and dash pepper. Coat lamb shanks on all sides in seasoned flour. Brown evenly in hot oil. Stir in onion and garlic; cook till tender but not brown. Add remaining ingredients; cook, covered, over low heat till tender, about 1 hour and 15 minutes. Turn meat once or twice during cooking. Skim excess fat from sauce before serving with meat. Makes 2 servings.

CHILIES RELLENOS BAKE

    ½ pound ground beef
    ¼ cup chopped onion
    1 4-ounce can green chilies
    2 ounces sharp process
      American cheese, shredded (½ cup)
    ¾ cup cold milk
    2 tablespoons all-purpose flour
    ¼ teaspoon salt
      Dash pepper
    2 beaten eggs
      Dash bottled hot pepper sauce

In skillet, brown beef and onion; drain off excess fat. Sprinkle meat with ¼ teaspoon salt and dash pepper. Split chilies lengthwise and remove seeds; spread open. Lay half of chilies on bottom of a shallow 1-quart baking dish. Sprinkle with cheese; top with meat mixture. Arrange remaining chilies over meat.

Gradually add milk to flour, stirring till smooth. Add salt, pepper, eggs, and hot pepper sauce; beat till smooth. Pour over casserole. Bake in moderate oven (350°) 45 to 50 minutes or till knife inserted just off center comes out clean. Pour off excess fat. Cool 5 minutes. Makes 2 or 3 servings.

CHILI FRANKS

    ½ cup narrow 1-inch long green
      pepper strips
    ¼ cup chopped onion
    1 tablespoon butter or margarine
    1 8-ounce can kidney beans
    ½ cup tomato sauce
    ¼ to ½ teaspoon chili powder
    3 frankfurters, sliced
    2 ounces sharp process American
      cheese, shredded (½ cup)
      Corn chips

In a saucepan, cook green pepper and onion in butter or margarine till tender but not brown. Add beans (with liquid), tomato sauce, chili powder, and franks. Cook, stirring occasionally, till hot. Add cheese; stir till melted. Serve over corn chips. Serves 2.

BARBECUE CHICKEN WINGS

- ¼ cup butter or margarine, melted
- ½ cup chili sauce
- 1 tablespoon lemon juice
- 1 teaspoon salt
- 1 teaspoon prepared mustard
- 1 teaspoon Worcestershire sauce
  Dash curry powder
- 8 chicken wings

Mix all ingredients except chicken. Pour over chicken wings in shallow baking dish. Bake at 350° for 50 minutes or till tender, turning two or three times. Makes 2 servings.

SALMON SCALLOP

- 1 7¾-ounce can salmon
  Dash pepper
  Dash dried dillweed
- ½ cup fine saltine cracker crumbs (14 crackers)
- 2 teaspoons lemon juice
- ⅓ cup milk
- ¼ cup chopped celery
- 1 tablespoon butter or margarine

Flake salmon (with liquid) into bowl, removing skin and bones. Stir in remaining ingredients except butter. Turn into 2-cup casserole. Dot with butter. Bake in moderate oven (350°) for 35 minutes. Makes 2 servings.

BEEF-STUFFED ONIONS

- 4 medium onions
- ½ pound ground beef
- 2 tablespoons catsup
- ¼ teaspoon salt
- 1 tablespoon grated Parmesan cheese
- 2 tablespoons quick-cooking rolled oats

Peel onions; cook in boiling salted water 20 to 30 minutes or till just tender. Drain and cool. Cut slice off top. Lift out centers, leaving shell intact. Chop enough of centers to make 2 tablespoons; add remaining ingredients; mix well. Fill onions; sprinkle with additional Parmesan. Place in greased baking dish. Bake at 375° about 30 minutes. Serves 2.

This easy-on-the budget casserole is tops in flavor. Sausage Kraut Bake sports a golden Parmesan cheese and potato topper.

SAUSAGE KRAUT BAKE

For speed, substitute instant mashed potatoes—

- 2 medium potatoes
- 1 8-ounce can (1 cup) sauerkraut, drained
- 1 tablespoon sliced green onion
- ½ pound bulk pork sausage
  • • •
- 2 tablespoons milk
- 1 tablespoon butter or margarine
- ¼ teaspoon salt
  Dash pepper
  • • •
- 2 tablespoons grated Parmesan cheese

Pare and cook potatoes. Meanwhile, combine sauerkraut and onion; place in 2- to 3-cup casserole. Brown sausage; drain; spoon over sauerkraut. Drain potatoes; mash with milk, butter, salt, and pepper. Spread over sausage; sprinkle with Parmesan cheese. Bake in hot oven (400°) for 25 to 30 minutes or till lightly browned. Makes 2 servings.

PENNYWISE EGG AND CHEESE DISHES

NOODLES PARMESAN

6 tablespoons butter, softened
1 3-ounce package cream cheese, softened
1 tablespoon snipped parsley
½ teaspoon dried basil, crushed
3 ounces thin noodles
½ clove garlic, minced
⅓ cup grated Parmesan cheese

Combine *2 tablespoons* butter, cream cheese, parsley, basil, dash salt, and dash pepper; blend. Stir in ⅓ cup boiling water; mix well. Keep warm. Cook noodles in boiling salted water; drain. Cook garlic in remaining butter 1 to 2 minutes; pour over hot noodles; toss. Add *half* the Parmesan cheese; toss lightly. Pile noodles on serving plate; spoon sauce over. Top with remaining Parmesan. Serves 2.

COTTAGE CHEESE OMELET

Beat 4 eggs till well mixed. Stir in ¼ teaspoon salt, dash pepper, 3 tablespoons milk, and ½ cup cottage cheese with chives. Melt 1 tablespoon butter or margarine in 8-inch skillet over medium heat; pour in egg mixture.

As omelet cooks, lift edges and tip pan so uncooked mixture flows under cooked portion. When underside is lightly browned and omelet is set, turn out. Serve immediately. Serves 2.

SPANISH EGGS AND RICE

1 8-ounce can (1 cup) Spanish rice
2 eggs
2 ounces sharp process American cheese, shredded (½ cup)

Spoon rice into 2 individual casseroles. Make depression in center of rice; carefully break egg into depression. Sprinkle ¼ cup cheese around edge of each casserole. Bake in moderate oven (350°) for 20 to 25 minutes or till eggs are desired doneness. Makes 2 servings.

EGGS FLORENTINE

Mix ½ 10-ounce package frozen chopped spinach, cooked and drained, with ¼ cup condensed Cheddar cheese soup. Spoon into 2 individual casseroles. Make depression in each; carefully break 1 egg into each depression.

Mix ¼ cup condensed Cheddar cheese soup with 1 teaspoon instant minced onion, ½ teaspoon prepared mustard, and 2 teaspoons milk; spoon over eggs and spinach. Top with ¼ cup crushed melba toast (3 slices) *or* croutons. Bake in moderate oven (350°) for 20 to 25 minutes or till eggs are set. Serves 2.

SPANISH DEVILED EGGS

2 tablespoons chopped onion
1 tablespoon chopped green pepper
1 tablespoon butter or margarine
1½ teaspoons all-purpose flour
1 8-ounce can (1 cup) tomatoes
½ teaspoon sugar
Deviled Eggs
¼ cup fine dry bread crumbs
1 teaspoon butter, melted

Cook onion and green pepper in 1 tablespoon butter till tender; blend in flour. Add tomatoes, sugar, dash salt, and dash pepper. Cook and stir till bubbly. Pour into 2 individual casseroles. Arrange 3 Deviled Egg halves in each. Combine crumbs and melted butter; sprinkle over. Bake in a hot oven (425°) for 10 minutes. Makes 2 servings.

Deviled Eggs: Halve 3 hard-cooked eggs lengthwise; remove yolks and mash. Blend in 2 tablespoons mayonnaise, ½ teaspoon vinegar, ½ teaspoon prepared mustard, dash salt, and dash pepper. Refill whites.

Brunch or lunch in a Spanish mood

Spanish Deviled Eggs bake in a peppy tomato sauce, topped with crumbs. A perfect trio with green salad and crusty bread.

Swirl and shake skillet all the while omelet cooks to keep egg from sticking.

With fork, stir egg out to edges of skillet, bringing cooked bits to center.

Tilt skillet over warmed plate so that you can roll the omelet onto plate.

FRENCH OMELET

  3 eggs
  1 tablespoon water
 ¼ teaspoon salt
     Dash pepper
     Dash mixed herbs (optional)
  1 tablespoon butter or margarine

With a fork, beat eggs, water, salt, pepper, and mixed herbs together till mixture is blended, but not frothy.

Heat an 8-inch skillet; add the butter or margarine—it should sizzle and brown lightly. Tilt pan to grease sides. Pour in egg mixture, leaving heat moderately high.

With fork tines up and parallel to skillet, rapidly stir through top of uncooked egg. Keep omelet an even depth. As you stir the uncooked egg back and forth out to edges, cooked bits will come to center. Shake pan continuously to keep omelet sliding.

The omelet should cook in 2 to 3 minutes. When egg is set but still shiny, remove skillet from heat. Fill center with sauteed mushrooms, if desired. Fold sides of omelet over filling; tilt pan and roll omelet onto warm serving plate. Makes 2 servings.

SPECIAL-DAY EGGS

  3 eggs
  3 tablespoons milk
     Dash *each* salt and pepper
  1 tablespoon chopped canned pimiento
  2 tablespoons butter or margarine
  1 2-ounce can chopped mushrooms, drained

        • • •

  1 large English muffin, split and toasted
  2 slices process American cheese

Slightly beat eggs; add milk, salt, pepper, and pimiento. Melt butter in small heavy skillet; add mushrooms; cook 1 minute. Add egg mixture. Cook over low heat, lifting and turning eggs with wide spatula, till eggs are cooked throughout but still moist and glossy.

Remove from heat at once. Spoon eggs over English muffin halves; top each with cheese slice. Broil 1 minute or till cheese just melts atop scrambled eggs. Makes 2 servings.

Lift and turn scrambled eggs so uncooked mixture flows to bottom of skillet.

CHEESE SCRAMBLED EGGS

Make Scrambled Eggs (opposite), adding 1½ ounces cream cheese, cut in pieces, to the uncooked egg-milk mixture.

POACHED EGGS

Fill a saucepan with water 3 to 4 inches deep; bring just to boiling. Stir the simmering water to make a swirl; then slip egg from sauce dish into the middle of the swirl. Turn heat down and cook egg 3 to 5 minutes, depending on desired doneness. Remove egg from water with slotted spoon. Serve on toast or an English muffin, split and toasted.

For best results when poaching eggs, follow motion of swirl with sauce dish so egg goes into water in same direction as swirl.

SCRAMBLED EGGS

In mixing bowl, beat 4 eggs, 3 tablespoons milk, ⅛ teaspoon salt, and dash pepper with fork. Heat 1 tablespoon butter in skillet till drop of water sizzles. Pour in egg mixture; turn heat to low. When egg starts to set, lift and turn cooked portion with wide spatula. Cook 5 to 8 minutes or till set but still moist and glossy. Makes 2 servings.

CHEESE RAMEKINS

> 3 ounces sharp process
> American cheese, shredded (¾ cup)
> 2 slightly beaten egg yolks
> 1 cup soft bread crumbs
> 1 cup milk, scalded
> 2 stiffly beaten egg whites

Reserve 2 tablespoons cheese. Mix remaining cheese, egg yolks, crumbs, and milk. Fold in egg whites. Turn into two 1½-cup casseroles. Top with reserved cheese. Bake at 325° for 35 to 40 minutes or till knife inserted off center comes out clean. Serve immediately. Serves 2.

Cheese Ramekins are like miniature souffles! You'll love the sharp cheese flavor and delicate texture for brunch or light supper.

BEST BURGERS

QUICK TOMATO BURGERS

½ pound ground beef
1 small tomato, cubed
2 tablespoons mustard-style hot dog relish
2 tablespoons mayonnaise
¼ teaspoon salt
Dash pepper
2 hamburger buns, split and toasted

Brown meat in skillet, stirring frequently. Add remaining ingredients except buns. Heat through. Serve over buns. Makes 2 servings.

GARLIC "STEAKBURGERS"

½ pound ground beef
2 cloves garlic, finely chopped
2 tablespoons butter or margarine
2 ½-inch slices French bread, toasted

Shape meat in 2 patties ½-inch thick. Cook garlic lightly in butter in skillet. Place patties in skillet. Cook 6 minutes on first side. Turn; cook 4 minutes or till done. Dash with salt and pepper. Drizzle butter from skillet on bread; top with patties. Serves 2.

SOUR CREAM BURGERS

½ pound ground beef
2 tablespoons chopped onion
¼ cup catsup
1 teaspoon vinegar
½ teaspoon salt
¼ teaspoon dry mustard
• • •
¼ cup dairy sour cream
2 hamburger buns, split and toasted

Brown ground beef with onion; drain off excess fat. Stir in catsup, vinegar, salt, and dry mustard. Cover and cook over low heat for 15 minutes. Stir in sour cream and heat, but do not boil. Serve over buns. Serves 2.

CHEESE-SAUCED BURGERS

½ pound ground beef
1 tablespoon butter or margarine
1 tablespoon all-purpose flour
¼ teaspoon dry mustard
½ cup milk
⅓ cup shredded process Swiss cheese
1 tablespoon dry sherry
2 slices bread, hamburger bun, French bread, *or* English muffin, toasted

Shape meat in 2 patties. Broil 3 inches from heat about 4 minutes on first side. Sprinkle with salt and pepper. Turn patties and broil 4 minutes more or to desired doneness. Season second side with salt and pepper.

Meanwhile, make cheese sauce: Melt butter; blend in flour and mustard. Add milk all at once. Cook and stir till sauce thickens and bubbles. Add cheese; stir till melted. Add wine; cook and stir 1 minute. Place patties on toast; top with sauce. Makes 2 servings.

DOUBLE VEGETABLE BURGERS

¼ pound ground beef
1 egg yolk
1 tablespoon milk
⅓ cup grated carrot
2 tablespoons finely chopped celery
1 tablespoon chopped green pepper
1 tablespoon finely chopped onion
1 teaspoon steak sauce
Dash garlic salt (optional)
Dash *each* salt and pepper
2 hamburger buns, split and toasted

Thoroughly combine all ingredients except buns; shape in 2 patties about ½-inch thick. Broil 3 to 4 inches from heat for 6 minutes on first side. Turn; broil 4 minutes more or to desired doneness.

Serve in hot toasted buns. Offer slices of tomato and cucumber. Makes 2 servings.

Giant burger boasts real pizza flavor! Broil the savory meat mixture atop a big slice of bread or toasted bun halves. Add mozzarella cheese and cherry tomatoes for a return trip to the broiler. Pizza Burger for Two makes a delicious and attractive lunch treat.

PIZZA BURGER FOR TWO

1   ¾-inch slice from large round
    loaf white bread *or* 2 hamburger
    buns, split
½   pound ground beef
2   tablespoons grated Parmesan
    cheese
2   tablespoons finely chopped onion
2   tablespoons chopped ripe olives
½   teaspoon salt
½   teaspoon dried oregano, crushed
¼   cup catsup
1   to 2 slices mozzarella cheese, cut
    in ½-inch strips
    Cherry tomatoes, halved

Toast bread or buns. Combine meat with next 6 ingredients and dash pepper; blend. Spread mixture on toasted bread. Broil 5 inches from heat 8 minutes or till done. Add cheese and cherry tomato halves; broil till cheese begins to melt, about 1 minute. Trim with cherry tomato and ripe olive. Serves 2.

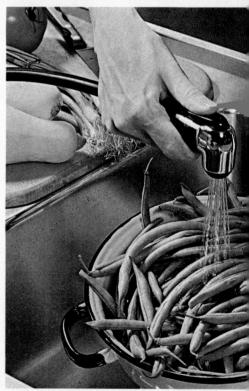

THE ABCs OF COOKING FOR TWO

Because many cooking-for-two situations involve young homemakers, we've collected some basic suggestions that will make the kitchen run smoothly and efficiently. The first step, of course, is to acquire a good set of cooking utensils and other kitchen tools. We've provided a list of basic utensils to guide your purchases. You'll find individual casseroles and small foilware pans especially useful.

Next comes grocery shopping. If you're new at this, we'll help you avoid some of the pitfalls and show you the best ways to care for and store meat and produce.

Since you may have limited storage space for food supplies, we've included a list of recipe substitutions—what to do if you don't have what the recipe calls for. There are also hints for the use of cheese plus a guide for herbs and wines so that you can serve expertly seasoned foods.

Upper right: Kitchen tongs are the perfect tool for holding and dipping many foods. Be sure to use tongs instead of a fork for turning broiled meats to avoid loss of natural juices. *Lower right:* A colander is especially useful for washing vegetables. Remember to wash and drain rather than soak fresh vegetables and fruits. *Upper left:* The wise cook saves time and extra dishwashing by measuring and then mixing right in the measuring cup. *Center left:* A rubber spatula makes a wonderful stirrer for cooked sauces because it gets into the "corners" of the pan. *Lower left:* Plastic bags have many uses in food preparation. Here the bag corrals dried bread slices being crushed for crumbs.

EQUIPPED TO COOK FOR TWO

Cooking utensils:

For top-of-the-range cooking, you'll find utensils available with a wide variety of features. You may want to choose some of the portable electric helpers, too.

covered 10-inch skillet
small 7- or 8-inch skillet
covered saucepans (1, 2, 4 to 6 quarts)
coffee maker
toaster

Kitchen tools:

can opener	utility slicer
grater or shredder	carving knife
pancake turner	colander
long-handled fork	potato masher
vegetable peeler	juicer
kitchen shears	long-handled spoon
pair of tongs	vegetable brush
2 paring knives	strainers, small
serrated knife	and medium

For measuring:

nested set of dry measuring cups
measuring cup for liquids
measuring spoons

For mixing:

rotary beater	electric mixer
set of mixing bowls	flour sifter
large wooden spoon	rubber spatula
rolling pin, cover	pastry cloth

For baking:

oblong pan (13x9x2)	loaf dish (8½x4½x2½)
round cake pans	tube pan
square pans	muffin pan
pie plates	custard cups
cookie sheets	jelly roll pan
wire cooling rack	casserole with cover
roasting pan, rack	pot holders, hot pads

Good features to shop for

A utensil should be balanced, have flat bottom, and straight sides to make best contact with cooking surface. A slight taper inside makes stirring easier. Handles should be comfortable to grasp, well fastened, and of nonheat-conducting material.

Guide for buying pans

Cooking for two—or twenty, for that matter—is more fun if you have the right pots and pans. Here are some guidelines to help you invest wisely:

• Choose the sizes of pans you need to hold the amount of foods you usually cook. Remember, it's more efficient to fill a pan to at least two-thirds its capacity.

• Every pan needs a cover, and it should fit securely. Cover knobs should be of nonheat-conducting material.

• Pick out versatile pieces that will do many jobs for you, such as cookers that serve at the table as well.

• Choose the best quality you can afford.

GROCERY SHOPPING FOR TWO

Helps for marketing

An important part of good meals for two is buying the right groceries for two. These pointers will help you organize your shopping, and save time and money at the store.

• Keep a memo pad handy in your kitchen; as you use the last of a staple, jot it down. Also, list "best buys" from the newspaper.

• Plan meals for the week ahead. This makes for variety in your menus and helps you take advantage of bargains. Remember to include a new food, a new seasoning, or a new way with an old favorite.

• Check the extras you'll need to buy and add to your memo pad.

• Now go over the list and group items as they are in the store—meats, baking supplies, etc. This avoids backtracking.

• You'll save time if you shop early in the day or during the middle of the week when stores are less crowded.

• Buy just what you have space to store and can use without waste.

• In-season plentifuls are better for the budget than those out-of-season temptations.

• Read labels—know what you're buying.

Basics to have on call

Here's a list of foods you can't cook without! It's also a good start-from-scratch grocery list for brides or for homemakers who have moved to a new location.

sugar, flour	salad oil
salt, pepper	pickles, olives
baking powder	prepared mustard
soda, yeast	Worcestershire sauce
coffee and/or tea	steak sauce, catsup
shortening	bread, rolls
butter, margarine	eggs
spices, herbs	meat, bacon
vanilla, chocolate	salad greens
cereal	vegetables, fruits
mayonnaise and/or	juices
salad dressing	milk, cream

Foods to keep on hand

Hurry-up meals, unexpected guests, change of plans, and "I'm hungrys" don't need to throw you if you keep some of these handy foods on your shelves. Remember also, a well-stocked cupboard always has the ingredients for a favorite company meal or two. Then you're set to meet any occasion.

packaged mixes—biscuit, cake, frosting, roll, cookie, pancake, pie crust, pudding
packaged dinners—macaroni, pizza, etc.
packaged herb-seasoned stuffing mix
rice, macaroni, spaghetti, noodles
dry soup, canned soup, bouillon cubes
canned meats—luncheon meat, ham, tuna, chicken, corned beef hash, spaghetti, beef stew, pork and beans
unflavored and fruit-flavored gelatin
canned breads (date-nut roll, Boston brown bread)
canned vegetables, fruits, juices
canned gravy or gravy mix
evaporated milk and/or nonfat dry milk
instant coffee, tea, cocoa, cream
raisins, dried prunes
maple-flavored syrup, corn syrup, honey, molasses
canned pie fillings
crackers, cookies
meat tenderizer
sundae toppings
jellies, jams, and preserves
cornstarch
nuts
marshmallows
cranberry sauce
peanut butter
soft drinks
cheese—American and cheese spread
dairy sour cream, cottage cheese
refrigerated biscuits and rolls
frozen soups and prepared dishes
ice cream and sherbet
frozen vegetables, fruits, juice concentrates
frozen meat, fish, seafood

FOOD IS MONEY— STORE IT RIGHT

Here are storage tips that will pay you big dividends in money and good flavor. A principle: *promptly* unpack groceries and store perishables as directed.

Fresh vegetables: Wash, drain, and dry greens; wrap or put in plastic bag; chill. Scrub carrots, celery, radishes, and green onions under cold water. Dispose of excess leaves and tops. Wrap or bag vegetables separately in moisture-vaporproof materials. Store dry onions, potatoes, and winter squash unwashed in dark cool place. Clean when ready to use.

Fresh fruits: Sort berries; spread on shallow pan or tray. Don't wash. Chill. Wash and stem before using. Ripen avocados, melons, and pears at room temperature; then refrigerate. Do not refrigerate bananas. Store fresh uncut pineapple in dark cool place. After cutting, wrap pineapple and chill in refrigerator.

Canned food leftovers: Cover and store in opened can for short period of time or transfer to covered refrigerator container.

Meat: For fresh meat, see below. Plan to use ground meat within 2 days, roasts—5 to 6 days, chops and steaks—3 days. Store cured and smoked meats in refrigerator in original wrap. Canned meats keep on the kitchen shelf, except for canned hams which are marked "Perishable; keep refrigerated."

For fresh chicken, turkey, or other poultry, store same as fresh meat below.

Fish: Wrap tightly; refrigerate.

Cheese: Wrap tightly and refrigerate. Chill cheese spreads in refrigerator once they're opened. Store strong-flavored cheeses in tightly covered jars; refrigerate.

Eggs: Store, covered, small end down in refrigerator. Don't wash till ready to use.

Dried fruits and nuts: Keep in covered jars or packages in cool, dry place. Nuts keep longer if stored in refrigerator.

Cookies: Soft and crisp kinds don't mix; store separately. Soft cookies stay moist when tightly covered. Crisp types of cookies keep well in jar with a loose-fitting lid.

Rule number one for any leftover: chill it fast! Spoon stuffing from chicken or turkey into refrigerator dish with cover. Wrap leftover poultry tightly in foil. Refrigerate.

Rewrap paper-wrapped fresh meat loosely with waxed paper; refrigerate. Store meat which has been prepackaged in moisture-vaporproof wrap 1 to 2 days in refrigerator.

LITTLE TIPS FOR BIG SUCCESSES

Grated and shredded—what's the difference? If you interpret grated lemon or orange peel to mean very fine particles, and shredded peel to mean small, long, narrow pieces—you score 100! When used in equal amounts, grated peel gives more flavor than shredded. However, you'll choose shredded peel for a pretty garnish. (If recipe calls for both fruit juice and grated or shredded peel, it's easier on the fingers if you first prepare the peel—then squeeze fruit for the juice.)

Chop, dice, and mince, are similar terms, yet there is a distinction. To chop, you will cut food in pieces about the size of peas. Diced food is cut in small cubes of uniform size and shape. Minced means very finely chopped. (Remember—if a recipe calls for minced onion, it is not the instant-type, dehydrated onion unless specifically stated. One tablespoon instant minced onion, being more concentrated in flavor, goes further than a tablespoon of fresh minced onion.)

Boiling and simmering are similar words, but are you sure of the difference? You've seen the phrase, "cook just till boiling" . . . this indicates bubbles come to the surface, where they break. Bubbles form rapidly throughout the mixture when it has reached a *full-rolling* or *hard boil*. If directions call for simmering, you'll use a lower temperature for cooking. Bubbles form at a much slower rate—and burst before reaching surface. (If temperature is too high and mixture boils rather than simmers, liquid will evaporate too fast.)

Beat, blend, stir, and cream—ever wonder about the proper translation? Beating makes a mixture creamy-smooth, or airy— you'll use a brisk whipping motion. To blend is simply to mix two or more ingredients till smooth and uniform. Stirring is mixing with a circular motion—around and around to combine ingredients till well blended or of uniform consistency. To cream is to beat with spoon or mixer till smooth. Shortening and sugar are creamed till light and fluffy.

Soft peaks or stiff peaks make a difference when beating egg whites. Take the case of a standard meringue. First, the recipe directs to beat egg whites to soft peaks. Here, the egg whites hold their shape when beaters are lifted, but the peaks droop a bit. Sugar is added gradually as you beat to stiff peaks. Peaks stand up straight, but are moist and glossy. You're now asked to *seal* meringue to pastry. Know how to manage that technique? This is simply spreading the meringue over the filling, touching the edge of the pastry all the way around, so as to seal out the air— important to prevent shrinking of meringue during baking time.

Fold in and cut in—do you know what these directions mean? You fold in new ingredients to a mixture that's beaten till light. Then air bubbles that make it fluffy won't be lost. Cut down through the mixture with spatula; go across bottom of bowl, up and over, close to surface. Turn bowl often for even distribution. Be gentle, but thorough. Cut in means to mix shortening with dry ingredients, using pastry blender or knives.

Saute, dredge, poach, and puree are terms that are often misinterpreted. To saute onion, for example, is to cook it quickly in butter, margarine, or other fat till tender. Coating meat with a flour mixture before browning, is dredging. To poach fresh fruit or fish steaks, simmer the food in hot liquid, watching to see that the food retains its shape. To puree is to sieve or blend cooked fruits or vegetables to make a smooth uniform mixture.

Baking pan or baking dish—there is a difference. A pan is metal; a dish is glass. The baking time may vary if a glass dish is used when a metal pan is specified, or when a pan is used instead of a dish.

Cool and chill mean two different things. Cool is to remove food from heat and let stand at room temperature. Chill is to refrigerate a certain time period.

Special tips to help make your vegetable salads the most successful yet

Shower leafy greens with cold water and then toss lightly in kitchen towel or paper towels to dry.

Store rinsed lettuce and other salad vegetables in crisper of refrigerator to keep them fresh and perky.

Salad tastes twice as refreshing if the plates or bowls are pre-chilled a few hours on refrigerator shelf.

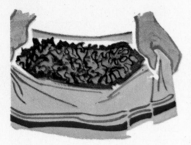 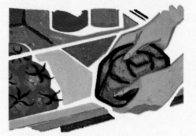 

IF YOU'RE OUT OF AN INGREDIENT ...

For best results, use what the recipe calls for. But for real emergencies, you'll appreciate the following ingredient substitution list. (A reminder: 1 tablespoon = 3 teaspoons.)

If you don't have . . . you can substitute		*If you don't have . . . you can substitute*	
1 cup cake flour	1 cup minus 2 tablespoons all-purpose flour	1 square unsweetened chocolate	3 tablespoons cocoa plus 1 tablespoon butter or margarine
1 tablespoon cornstarch (for thickening)	2 tablespoons flour *or* 4 teaspoons quick-cooking tapioca	1 small fresh onion	1 tablespoon instant minced onion, rehydrated
1 whole egg	2 egg yolks (in custard)	1 teaspoon dry mustard	1 tablespoon prepared mustard
½ cup butter or margarine	½ cup shortening plus ¼ teaspoon salt	1 teaspoon baking powder	¼ teaspoon soda plus ½ cup sour milk to replace ½ cup liquid
1 cup whole milk	½ cup evaporated milk plus ½ cup water *or* 1 cup reconstituted nonfat dry milk plus 2 teaspoons butter	1 cup tomato juice	½ cup tomato sauce plus ½ cup water
1 cup sour milk *or* buttermilk	1 tablespoon lemon juice or vinegar plus sweet milk to make 1 cup (let stand 5 minutes)	1 cup catsup *or* chili sauce	1 cup tomato sauce plus ½ cup sugar and 2 tablespoons vinegar (for use in cooked mixtures)

GUIDELINES FOR SMART COOKS

- Keep on hand food items you use often. Group similar items on shelves. This speeds selection and you can see at a glance when it's time to buy replacements.
- Organize your refrigerator so there's a certain space for leftovers. Then you can easily see what's on hand and what needs to be used promptly—thus cutting food waste.
- Mentally check your menu plans for the day. Be sure you don't have too many last-minute tasks. Then, think through your preparation schedule, planning to *dovetail* activities whenever possible.
- Learn to read recipes carefully *before* you begin. Do you have all the ingredients? Is there something you should do first—melt chocolate, beat eggs, make pastry?
- Turn on oven, if needed, when you start preparation, so it will reach correct temperature by the time food is ready to be baked.

- Assemble ingredients and utensils *before* beginning recipe—you'll save time and effort!
- If more than one menu item calls for chopped food, do all your chopping at once. Remember, too, chopped onion and green pepper freeze well for use later on.
- Use kitchen shears to snip parsley, chives, dates, etc. It's quicker than a knife.
- In planning your menu, remember flavor, temperature, and texture contrasts keep meals from becoming humdrum. For example, serve a crisp cold salad with hot soup.
- Serve hot foods hot, cold foods cold!
- A smart cook plans a surprise in every meal—some little extra, like a special muffin, an unusual relish, a tasty trim, a favorite dessert served in a new way.
- Clean up as you go. Wash utensils as you finish using them; soak stubborn pans. Take care of leftovers right away.

HOW TO USE HERBS

When first experimenting, easy does it! Use just enough herb to heighten natural food flavors. One strongly seasoned dish per meal is generally a good rule of thumb.

- Start with $\frac{1}{4}$ teaspoon dried herbs to four servings, or to one pound of meat, poultry, or fish, or to 2 cups sauce or vegetables.
- If substituting fresh herbs for dried, use 3 or 4 times as much fresh herbs.
- Measure dried herbs; then crush them in the palm of your hand before adding—this helps hasten the flavor release.
- Add herbs at the same time as salt and pepper to meats, vegetables, and sauces.
- In long-cooking foods, such as stews, add herbs during last half hour of cooking.
- Add herbs to juices or cold sauces ahead of time—let stand overnight if possible.
- Many herbs are compatible, so don't hesitate to use several herbs together.

Try some of these ideas for herbs, then experiment on your own and taste the delicious difference that herbs make.

- Basil is a natural for tomato and potato dishes. Try $\frac{1}{4}$ teaspoon for each cup of tomato juice for a quick appetizer.
- When making potato salad, cook potatoes with a bay leaf and some onion.
- Sprinkle caraway seed over coleslaw.
- Add a dash of chili powder to corn.
- Chives are great in cottage and cream cheeses, and also in scrambled eggs.
- Add curry powder to deviled eggs.
- Oregano gives character to meat loaf, stew, chili, and tomato mixtures.
- Spark seafood and chicken dishes with tarragon. Also gives tang to tartar sauce.
- Thyme is popular for soups and chowders.
- Sage is best liked with pork and in stuffings for turkey and chicken.

HINTS ON WINE

Cooking with wine can be creative but it's not a case of "if a little is good, more is better!" The flavor of wine is meant to be a subtle accent, enhancing the natural food flavors. When wine is heated the alcohol (and, happily, most of the calories) evaporates leaving only the distinctive wine flavor.

Feel free to substitute one wine for another in a recipe but choose a similar wine from the same group in the chart below. In general, dryer wines are used in main dishes, sweeter wines in desserts and sauces. Sparkling wines are not often used in cooking because they would rapidly lose their effervescence—which is what makes them distinctive.

You don't need a cellar to store wine properly. Just keep bottles away from direct sunlight, extreme temperatures, or vibration. Store corked bottles on their sides so liquid covers bottom of cork, keeping it moist. The ideal temperature for storing wines is a constant one between 50 and 60 degrees, but 60 to 70 degrees is fine for a few months.

Once opened, table wines keep several days if tightly closed and refrigerated. Dessert and appetizer wines keep well for a month.

If you are just starting your home wine supply, you'll be prepared for any occasion if you select one wine from each of the five groups in the serving chart below.

WINES	FOODS	Ideal Serving and Storing TEMPERATURES
Appetizer Wines Sherry (dry to sweet) Vermouth (dry, sweet) Flavored wines Special natural wines	**All Appetizers** canapes, bouillon	45-50 degrees except: Sherry—60-70 degrees Dry Vermouth (serve over ice)
Red Table Wines Claret (dry) Red Burgundy (dry) Rose (pink, dry to sweet) Red Chianti (dry) Vino Rosso (semisweet)	**Hearty Foods** steak, roast game, roast, steak ham, pork, veal cheese, egg dishes, spaghetti	60-70 degrees Rose—45-50 degrees
White Table Wines Chateau Rhine Wine (dry to semisweet) White Chianti (dry to semisweet) Light Muscat (dry to sweet) White Burgundy (dry) Chablis (dry) Sauterne (dry to sweet) Semillon	**Light Foods** chicken, turkey lamb, veal seafoods shellfish	45-50 degrees or: refrigerate one to two hours to chill
Dessert Wines Port (sweet) Tawny Port (sweet) White Tokay (sweet) Cream or sweet Sherry Muscatel (sweet)	**All Desserts** sweets, nuts fruit, after coffee	60-70 degrees

Sparkling Wines
Sparkling Burgundy
    (red, semisweet to sweet)
Sparkling Muscat (sweet)
Sparkling Rose
    (dry to semisweet)
Champagnes
    (gold or pink)
    (Brut—very dry)
    (Sec—semidry)
    (Demi-Sec)
	All Occasions and Foods	40-45 degrees or:
		refrigerate one to
		two hours to chill

WAYS WITH CHEESE

When cooking with cheese, keep in mind that high temperatures or prolonged cooking may toughen the cheese or cause it to look stringy or curdled. For this reason, cheese should be added near the end of cooking. Process cheese is somewhat more tolerant of heat than the natural forms. Remember that once a cheese is melted, it is cooked.

The mold which may develop on cheese is not harmful. Scrape mold off surface before using. Grate ends or hard pieces of cheese and store in tightly covered jar. Use for garnish or in recipes calling for grated cheese.

For peak flavor, let all cheeses (except cottage cheese and cream cheese) stand at room temperature 30 minutes before serving.

Discover the flavor delights of a variety of cheeses. One of the best ways to do this is to adopt the European custom of fruit and cheese for dessert. For a start, try some of the following combinations:

String cubes of brick or muenster cheese with balls of cantaloupe or honeydew melon on skewers. Spread cream cheese on crackers and top with slices of preserved kumquats.

In the picture below, Cheddar or Swiss cheese is teamed with fresh apple or pear wedges or fresh cherries. "Sails" of Camembert and wedges of Gouda pair with orange sections, peach slices, or tart plums. Liederkranz and blue cheese accompany Tokay and seedless green grapes. Pass assorted crackers.

INDEX